TOWARDS A NEW PARADIGM IN HIGHER EDUCATION

TOWARDS A NEW PARADIGM IN HIGHER EDUCATION

Edited by
ASHOK CELLY

PUBLICATIONS

KALPAZ PUBLICATIONS
DELHI-110052

Towards A New Paradigm in Higher Education

ISBN: 81-7835-614-7

Published in 2008 in India by
Kalpaz Publications
C-30, Satyawati Nagar,
Delhi-110052
E-mail: kalpaz@hotmail.com
Phone : 9212729499

Laser Type Setting by: Quick Media, Delhi
Printed at : Vishal Kaushik Printers Delhi

CONTENTS

PREFACE

My interest in education dates back to April, 1972 when the *Hindustan Times* published my article 'To Hell with Public Schools'. Not only was it prominently placed, it also evoked a tremendous response. There was a spate of letters to the Editor supporting or attacking my position. There were even some articles in response to it and not just in *HT*. Such a thing doesn't happen these days.

Well, this happy accident seemed to decide my main interest for years to come apart from teaching undergraduates of course. I began to read everything on education that came my way and also to write on some aspect of it once in a while. Eventually I chose to focus on what is known as higher education partly because of my direct involvement in it and partly because educationists like Prof. Krishna Kumar and Prof. Anil Sadgopal have done excellent work in the field of school education.

Perhaps the most striking feature of our higher education is our extraordinary dependence on the west. The books that we read are all in English and largely published abroad. A foreign degree is still the ticket to success and prestige, and being published in a foreign journal is the dream of every Indian scholar. In fact, our subservience to the west has increased after independence. We had won our political independence but not Swaraj as Nauroji, Ranade, Tagore and other public intellectuals envisaged it. Swaraj is not to be understood in a narrowly patriotic sense of 'our country is the best'. Swaraj is essentially liberation from the great superstition of our times that there is just one route to development—that of the west; there is just one model of civilization—that of the west; and there is just one mode of knowledge—that of the west. Above all, Swaraj is the capacity to think independently and to find indigenous solutions to our problems.

During the course of my exploration I discovered kindred spirits—social scientists, philosophers and creative writers who had thought on similar lines. Their writings deepened my perceptions, and strengthened/modified my formulations. Interestingly enough none of them could be described as a professional educationist. We had indeed made a fetish of specialization, and in the process knowledge had been fragmented by "narrow domestic walls". The conviction grew upon me that if they are brought together, they will have a greater impact. Hence this book. Hopefully, it would interest not only students of education but also those pursuing sociology, political science, economics etc.

During this process, I received valuable assistance from several friends and colleagues. I would particularly like to thank Dr. A.L. Khanna, Prof. R.K. Agnihotri and Mr. Dilip Basu. I would also like to thank Mr. V.P. Singh who presented me a copy of Lohia's *Interval During Politics*. Finally, a word of gratitude for my wife Aruna who created just the right ambience for work of this nature.

ACKNOWLEDGEMENTS

I am deeply grateful to the following for permission to use the copyright material:

Leela Dube for permission to reprint Prof. S.C. Dube's "Indigenization of Social Sciences" from *S.C. Dube on Crisis and Commitment in Social Sciences*, (ed. Yogesh Atal, Abhinav Publications, New Delhi, 1983); V.K. Sinha, the Editor of *New Quest* for Daya Krishna's "Encounter between Civilizations" (*New Quest* 125, Sept-Oct 1997); Gopal Krishan the Editor of *Man and Development* for P.C. Joshi's "Countering Aupaniveshik Mansikta" *(Man and Development*, Vol. XIX, No. 1, March 1997); J.P.S. Uberoi for his article "Science and Swaraj" from *Contributions to Indian Sociology* (n.s., 1968, 2) and Bhola Prasad Singh the trustee of Dr. Rammanohar Lohia Samta Nyas, Hyderabad for "On Scheme of Research at Indian Universities" from *Interval during Politics* (ed. K.S. Karanth, Sindhu Publications, Bombay, 1987).

—Editor

LIST OF CONTRIBUTORS

K.C. Bhattacharya

One of India's greatest philosophers. Known for his works *Studies in Philosophy* and *The Subject as Freedom*. Was Principal of Hooghly College, Bengal when he delivered his famous discourse on "Swaraj In Ideas."

Rabindranath Tagore

Bengali poet, playwright, novelist and short story writer. Was also a great social and educational thinker of which "An Eastern University" is some evidence. He founded Visva-Bharati in 1921 – a university where "visva bharati ek needam."

Daya Krishna

An eminent philosopher of contemporary India. Was Professor of Philosophy at University of Rajasthan, Jaipur. His published works include *The Nature of Philosophy, Modern Logic Its Relevance in Philosophy* and *India's Intellectual Traditions* – the last being an edited work.

S.C. Dube

One of India's leading social scientists. Taught Political Science at Nagpur, Lucknow and Sociology at Osmania, London and Cornell. Some of his important books are *Indian Village, India's Changing Villages* and *Manav aur Sanskriti* (Hindi).

P.C. Joshi

Former Director of Institute of Economic Growth. Known in India and abroad for his studies in land reforms and agrarian change in India. His other areas of interest are economic thought of Gandhi and Nehru and Culture and Communication. He was also the Chairman of Committee for Software Planning for Doordarshan.

J.P.S. Uberoi

Was Professor of Sociology at Delhi School of Economics, His important published works are : *Religion, Civil Society* and *The State – A Study of Sikhism* and *The Other Mind of Europe: Goethe as a Scientist.*

Rammanohar Lohia

The well-known socialist leader and thinker could find time for things other than politics as the essay in this volume shows. His book *Gandhi, Marx and Socialism* is a work of great intellectual merit.

Ashok Celly

Was Reader in English, Rajdhani College, University of Delhi. Has authored a book entitled *Emily Bronte, D.H. Lawrence and the Black Horse* and edited D.H. Lawrence's *Sons and Lovers*. He has also contributed articles on cultural and educational issues to leading dailies like *The Times of India, Hindustan Times* and *Indian Express.*

INTRODUCTION

Ashok Celly

"There is so much I don't want to know. Wisdom puts a limit even to knowledge". *(Nietzsche)*

In the year 1592, Francis Bacon the well-known British thinker and essayist declared, "I confess that I have taken all knowledge to be my province".[1] Bacon's boast could well be described as the credo of the Renaissance in particular and the modern west in general, for the ideal of infinite knowledge seems to have ruled the consciousness of the western world ever since and continues to do so to this day.

What precisely is the ideal and what are its implications? One, it makes knowledge the supreme value of human existence. The more we know the better it is, for knowledge *per se* is viewed as the panacea for human ills. Knowledge is the difference between sick and sane society, unhappy and happy existence. As Nicholas Maxwell observes:

> "The view that rational inquiry ought to help enhance the quality of human life by, in the first instance, improving knowledge is, one might say, the official basic creed of the whole scientific/academic enterprise. The view can be traced back at least to Francis Bacon, and perhaps back to the

ancient Greeks. It has been almost unthinkingly taken for granted by almost everyone associated with the development of science, scholarship, universities and education in the western world and elsewhere. As a result the view is now firmly built into the whole intellectual institutional structure of the scientific/academic enterprise."[2]

It all started with Bacon one of the pioneers of the scientific method. Bacon (and later Galileo and Newton) was primarily concerned with the scientific knowledge - knowledge based on observation and experiment - of the natural world. Seeking inspiration from Bacon the *philosophes* Diderot, Voltaire, Montesquien and others extended it to the study of man and society. This meant collection and classification of knowledge in various fields and its finest fruit was a ten-volume *Encyclopaedia* edited by Diderot and d'Alembert. Diderot's declaration regarding its aims is also an affirmation of the Renaissance - Enlightenment faith in the primacy of knowledge implying a causal connection between knowledge and virtue/happiness:

> The aim of an Encyclopaedia is to assemble the knowledge scattered over the face of the earth to explain its general plan to the men with whom we live, and to transmit it to those who will come after us, so that the labours of the past centuries may not be useless to future times; so that our descendants, by becoming better informed, may in consequence be happier and more virtuous......[3]

Secondly, the knowledge thus acquired was objective, that is, morally neutral. This had something to do with the famous Cartesian dualism. Descartes the French thinker and mathematician tended to divide reality into 'thinking substance' and 'extended substances', mind and matter, fact and value, objective reality and subjective feelings and desires. The Cartesian schism decisively influenced the Renaissance—Enlightenment philosophy of knowledge. Objective knowledge was privileged and divorced from values and feelings. To quote Maxwell again, "Cartesian dualism divides up reality into two sharply distinct worlds: on the one hand the objective world of fact, matter, physical reality; on the other hand, the subjective world of mind, consciousness, personal experience, value. Once this view is accepted (as it was at one time by most scientists in one form or another), it becomes natural to suppose that rational inquiry, science, will reflect in its overall character the sharp split between fact and value, objective reality and subjective feelings and desires...."[4]

There can be no denying that there was a massive expansion of knowledge in all fields as a consequence but it also led to dehumanisation and nihilism. Nietzsche the *enfant terrible* of the western world had the clairvoyance to see the fatal consequences of the Renaissance—Enlightenment ideal and recognised the need to delimit knowledge. "There is so much I don't want to know. Wisdom puts a limit even to knowledge",[5] he declared. He tried to restore sanity to the heady intellectual adventure of the western man by reminding his peers that knowledge must serve life, not *vice versa.* "Is life to dominate knowledge and science, or is knowledge to dominate life? Which of these two forces is the higher and more decisive? There can be no doubt: life is the higher, the dominating force, for knowledge which annihilated life would have annihilated itself with it. Knowledge presupposed life and thus has in the preservation of life the same interest as any creature has in its own continued existence."[6]

The Baconian - Enlightenment emphasis on desirability of knowing all that can be known resulted in an explosion of knowledge, something that mankind (or its scientific/scholastic establishment) couldn't cope with. It was a case of knowledge overwhelming the knower as Nietzsche had warned. The Faustian adventure which seemed to promise so much power and freedom in fact landed the western man in a *cul de sac.* Also, the pursuit of objective, that is, morally neutral knowledge came to be divorced from human ends and became an autonomous, alienated pursuit. The true (Satyam) came to be divorced from the good (Shivam), and its most awesome expression was the Bomb. Thus, the apparently glorious ideal of the pursuit of knowledge regardless of where it would take us led to the Bomb and the blind alley!

With the introduction of western learning in India following the famous Macaulay minute, we in India also imbibed the Baconian - Enlightenment ideal.

The same thing happened in other third world countries which were colonised by the west. This was disabling for the third world countries in general and a country like India in particular which has more than three thousand years of cultural history. For the Baconian ideal in practice meant the desirability, nay the necessity, of assimilating all western knowledge. The reverse, i.e., their western counterparts acquiring oriental knowledge didn't hold true. Apart from the daunting enormity of this enterprise, it meant for the most part an engagement with ideas and issues that were not central to our socio-cultural existence[6]. Also, it meant joining a ratrace in which we were doomed to be political laggards. How often one hears of catching up with the west? The harsh truth is that in this race the west having had a head-start is bound to be streets ahead of us. C.T. Kurien's observations in the 1968 Symposium on the Relevance of Social Sciences in Contemporary Asia underline at once the excessive dependence of the Indian/Asian social scientist on the west and the skewed nature of his intellectual engagement. Kurien observes.

> We are neither Asians nor scientists. Our knowledge about the problems of our societies is largely bookish and books that we read are merely from the west.... We are beggars, all of us - we sneak under many an academic table to gather the crumbs under them.[7]

Social scientists from other Asian countries also agonised over the strangle hold of western concepts and called for a truly creative engagement with their own culture and society.[8]

This was in the year 1968, but has the situation substantially changed for the better? Prabhat Patnaik, for instance, in an essay that he contributed to *D. School* attributed the failure of Delhi School of Economics to the lack of "collective arrogance".[9] Patnaik's choice of words may be a little unfortunate but one can hardly quarrel with his basic formulation. In fact, the malaise he detects in *D. School* characterises the whole enterprise of higher education in India, that is, the utter lack of belief in themselves as a community of scholars to pursue knowledge independent of their counterparts in the west. However, Patnaik is reluctant to face the fact that the lack of belief in themselves— "collective arrogance" as he puts it - is inevitable given our intellectual orientation. To put it plainly, if our heroes are Arrows and Solows, if we subscribe to western concepts and paradigms, economics or for that matter any social science will remain 'a scary domain' and the inevitable conclusion will be '... to really learn economics we had to go there'.[10]

The dominance of western concepts and paradigms was evident, as S.C. Dube the eminent sociologist has shown convincingly, in the rejection of tradition and history by social anthropologists under the influence of Malinowski and Radcliff - Brown and then their zestful acceptance when Louis Dumont made a strong case for linking Indology and sociology or anthropology.[11] It could also be seen in the preoccupation with an exclusive economic model of development with its GNP fixation and mindless adherence to the capitalist notion that man is a *homo economicus* driven by greed and envy. A notion which is essentially a product of the bourgeois west and only applicable to a tiny segment of the middle class here. The crippling hold of the western paradigms could also be seen in the radical intellectual's indifference to caste as a sociological category perhaps as a mark of devotion to Karl Marx. The kind of liberating scepticism that marked Malibub Ul Haq's approach who posed the question. 'Of what use is conventional economics to us?' was rarely seen even in elite institutions like D School and JNU. Amartya Sen was an exception but then he was steeped in the rich humanistic culture of Tagore's Shantiniketan which presumably liberated him from the myopia of specialisation on the one hand and the dominance of western world-view on the other.

It is not that nobody in Indian recognised this malady—the ills that plagued the academia. Tagore's plea for "An Eastern University"—a seminal educational text in my opinion—was an attempt to relocate the intellectual centre of gravity here. In his essay Tagore gives expression to his deep sense of anguish over the absence of a centre of learning centrally concerned with the study of India's cultural and intellectual heritage. He observes, "In the whole length and breadth of India there is not a single university established in the modern time where a foreign or an Indian student can properly be acquainted with the best products of the Indian mind. For that we have to cross the sea and knock at the doors of France and Germany. Educational institutions in our country are India's alms-bowl of knowledge, they lower our intellectual self-respect..."[12]

Then there was M.G. Ranade the eminent jurist and leader from western India who tried to liberate our social sciences from the vice-like grip of the Anglo-Saxon model by "reminding Indian social scientists that within the west itself models other than the English economic model and thought system existed as a correction to the gaps, deficiencies and onesidedness of English and practice."[13] Similarly, Lohia the radical socialist thinker from the north, despite his pressing political concerns, pleaded for greater relevance in university research pointing out that theories of Adam Smith and Keynes were essentially British in nature.[14]

There were voices of protest in the academia as well. K.C. Bhattacharya in a lecture delivered as early as 1930 raised his voice against cultural subjection and made a plea for "Swaraj in Ideas". By cultural subjection Bhattacharya meant a state "when one's traditional cast of ideas and sentiments is superseded without comparison or competition by a new cast representing an alien culture which presses one like a ghost."[15] He passionately opposed mindless acceptance of western ideas and made a plea for "discovering our own self"[16] for only then there will be distinctly Indian estimates of though and culture.

More recently another eminent philosopher Daya Krishna pointed out that an unhappy consequence of the intellectual dominance of the west is that we feel "embarassed" about our ignorance of even a second-rate western thinker while our counterparts in the west are not bothered about even our first-rate thinkers.[17] Social scientists who have made significant contributions to indigenization of knowledge—freeing it from western paradigms/concepts and relating it to socio-cultural milieu—are S.C. Dube, P.C. Joshi and J.P.S. Uberoi. Dube and Joshi have authored books in Hindi and thus in a sense moved from theory to praxis. J.P.S. Uberoi detects the same malady in the field of natural science, namely, its dependence on the west in the name of cosmoplitanism. Dismissing "scientific internationalism as a bridge of illusion'[17] oberoi suggests that there is a direct causal connection between the colonial tie and the lack of originality. "Until we can concentrate on decolonialization (sic), learn to nationalize our problems and take our poverty seriously, we shall continue[18] to be *both colonial and unoriginal*'. (italics mine)

However, all this did not amount to a groundswell, an intellectual Movement. Perhaps they were isolated efforts and needed to be welded together by an alternative epistemology. [The Marxists did have an epistemology of sorts but it was tied a little too narrowly to political action. And even there it leaned too heavily on Russia or China]. If only we had taken the cue from somebody like Nietzsche, if we had the courage to question the Baconian-Enlightenment ideal of knowing more and more as the means of individual fulfilment and social progress, things could have been different. Our socio-cultural needs and aspiration would have determined our academic priorities rather than the monstrous Baconian ideal which made us perennial laggards or 'beggars picking up crumbs' as Kurien noted with great anguish. Here our humanists, i.e., philosophers, litterateurs and, above all, our historians had a role to play, for only in humanities are we centrally concerned with the questions: what are we? And what do we want to be? But, sad to say, our humanists were quite content to live in the pigeonholes of their specialisation abandoning their holistic calling. The mammoth expansion of knowledge, one might contend, made specialisation necessary. But specialisation was not recognised as a necessity, a necessary evil. Instead it was glorified. It led to a distortion of perspective. For no humanist worth his salt can be contented with what Arnold Toynbee once described as 'a worm's view'. He must always try to see the underlying connection between apparently disconnected fragments of knowledge. In other words he must perform the role of an intellectual. Not just transcend the boundaries of a discipline but also that of a culture, in this case the western culture. May be, by bringing together litterateurs, philosophers, social scientists and political activists on one platform we could take a step, however small, in the right direction.

One might legitimately ask, "what is the relevance of this project in the era of globalisation? Also, how is it different from the Hindutva dream of reviving the past?" It is true that the world has become a global village, to use the hackneyed phrase, thanks to the communication revolution. Does it mean we must give up our cultural identity and become imitation Yankees? In fact, in the era of globalisation the quest for cultural identity is even more imperative for cultural uniformity breeds alienation which in turn triggers a fundamentalist backlash as happened in Iran. Globalisation must not negate cultural diversity.

Secondly, to question the dominance of western knowledge and to plead for an acquaintance with the best products of Indian culture is not to endorse the saffron line. Nothing can be more ridiculous than to view Tagore and other thinkers included here as representing the Hindutva viewpoint. The vital difference between the Saffron brigade and the Swarajists, if one may use this term, is that the former mindlessly glorifies the past while the latter critiques it and incorporates what is vital and living in it. Also, he does not take a narrow sectarian view of the past but recognises and celebrates the contributions made by others, that is, Buddhists, Jains, Sikhs and Muslims etc. to Indian culture and society.

References

1. From a letter to Lord Burghley, cited from *The Cambridge Companion to Bacon,* ed. Markku Pettonen (Cambridge University Press, 1996), p. 5.
2. From *Knowledge to Wisdom* (Basil Blackwell, Oxford, 1984), p. 2.
3. Andrews, Stuart, *Eighteenth Century Europe: The 1680s to 1815* (Longmans, London 1965), p. 71.
4. From *Knowledge to Wisdom,* p. 12.
5. Twilight of the Idols from *Twilight of the Idols* and the Anti-Christ, trans R.J.Hollingdale (Penguin, Harmondsworth, 1968), p. 23.
6. On the uses and advantages of history for life' in *Untimely Meditations*, trans. R.J. Hollingdale (Cambridge. Cambridge University Press, 1983), p. 78.
7. Cited in "Social Sciences for the Eighties", *S.C. Dube on Crisis and Commitment In Social Sciences,* ed. Yogesh Atal (New Delhi Abhinav Publications, 1983), p. 83.
8. The other scholars are Espiritu, A. Caesar from Philippines and Yamaoka, Kikuo from Japan. See "Social Sciences for the Eighties" in *S.C. Dube on Crisis and Commitment in Social Sciences.*
9. "Delhi School Days", *D School* (OUP, Delhi, 1995), ed. Dharma Kumar & Dilip Mookherjee, p. 118.
10. *Ibid.,* p. 117.
11. "Indigenization of The Social Sciences", *S.C. Dube On Crisis and Commitment In Social Sciences,* p. 73.
12. *Selections from the Works of Rabindranath Tagore* (Macmillan and Co., Bombay, 1946), p. 65.
13. Cited in P.C. Joshi's "Countering Aupniveshik Mansikta: Swaraj and Swadesh in Indian Social Science". *Man and Development,* Vol. XIX, No. 1, March 1997, p. 15.

14. "Adam Smith had the genius to equate international trade with geographical division of labour, a primarily British equation but one that ruled the mind of the world for a hundred years and more. J.M. Keynes had again the genius to add the concept of ful employment to this equation, another British equation, but one that is currently ruling the mind of the English speaking world". Cited from "On schemes of research at Indian Universities", *Intervals During Politics* (Lohia Library-3, Sindu Publications, Bombay, 1987), p. 55.
15. "Swaraj in Ideas", *Four Indian Critical Essays,* ed. Sisirkumar Ghose (Jijnasa Calcutta, 1977), p. 13.
16. *Ibid.*, p. 14.
17. "Encounters Between Civilizatons," New Quest 125, Sept. Oct 1997, p. 265.
18. *Contributions to Indian Sociology* (n.s.) 1968. 2, p. 120.
19. *Ibid.*, p. 123.

1

SWARAJ IN IDEAS*

K.C. Bhattacharya

In addition to political domination, there is domination - more subtle, less conscious - in the sphere of culture and ideas Bhattacharya calls it cultural subjection. Cultural subjection may be seen to manifest itself "when one's traditional cast of ideas and sentiments is superseded without comparison or competition by a new cast representing an alien culture." When a person can shake himself free from this subjection - "slavery of the spiit" in Bhattacharya's phrase - he experences a "rebirth", a "Swaraj in Ideas." As things are - tragically enough they are not substantially different from what they were in 1929 when Bhattacharya delivered this lecture - we have our grounding in Western culture and then "peer into our ancient culture as a

---

*From *Four Indian Critical Essay,* ed. Sisirkumar Ghose (Jijnasa : Calcutta 1977)

curiosity and with the attitude of a foreign oriental scholar." And even though we primarily devote our time and energy to their pursuit, one canot really say there is intelligent assimilation of western ideas. For one rarely comes across distinctly original India contributions to philosophy, literary criticism and social sciences. Bhattacharya warns against "rootless universalism" and emphasises the culture-specific nature of ideas and ideals. At the same time Bhattacharya is not unaware of the other danger, namely, "unthinking glorification of everything in our culture."—Editor.]

We speak today of Swaraj or self-determination in politics. Man's domination over man is felt in the most tangible form in the political sphere. There is however a subtler domination exercised in the sphere of ideas by one culture on another, a domination all the more serious in the consequence, because it is not ordinarily felt. Political subjection primarily means restraint on the outer life of a people and although it tends gradually to sink into the inner life of the soul, the fact that one is conscious of it operates against the tendency. So long as one is conscious of a restraint, it is possible to resist it or to bear it as a necessary evil and to keep free in spirit. Slavery begins when one ceases to feel the evil and it deepens when the evil is accepted as a good. Cultural subjection is ordinarily of an unconscious character and it implies slavery from the very start. When I speak of cultural subjection, I do not mean the assimilation of an alien culture. That assimilation need not be an evil; it may be positively necessary for healthy progress and in any case it does not mean a lapse of freedom. There is cultural subjection only when one's traditional cast of ideas and sentiments is superseded without comparison or competition by a new cast representing an alien culture which possesses one like a ghost. This subjection is slavery of the spirit: when a person can shake himself free from it, he feels as though the scales feel from his eyes. He experiences a rebirth and that is what I call Swaraj in Ideas.

In these days when our political destinies are in the melting pot, one is tempted to express a doubt—till now vaguely felt but suppressed as uncultured—how far generally we have assimilated our 'Western' education and how far it has operated as an obsession. Certainly there has been some sort of assimilation—at least by some of us—but even of them it may be asked whether the alien culture has been accepted by them after a full and open-eyed struggle had been allowed to develop between it and their indigenous culture. It is admitted today—what was not sufficiently recognized in the earlier days of our Western education—that we had an indigenous culture of a high degree of development, the comparative value of which cannot be said to have been yet sufficiently appraised. Under the present system we generally receive Western culture in the first instance and then we sometimes try to peer into our ancient culture as a curiosity and with the attitude of foreign oriental scholars and yet we say that this ancient culture of ours is no curiosity. Many of our educated men do not know and do not care to know much of this indigenous culture of ours, and when they seek to know, they do not feel, as they ought to feel, that they are discovering their own self.

There is no gainsaying the fact that this Western culture - which means an entire system of ideas and sentiments - has been simply imposed on us. I do not mean that it has been imposed on unwilling minds; we ourselves asked for this education, and we feel, and perhaps rightly, that it has been a blessing in certain ways, I mean only that it has not generally been assimilated by us in an open-eyed way with our old-world Indian mind. That Indian mind has simply lapsed, in most cases for our educated men, and has subsided below the conscious level of culture. It operates still in the persisting routine of their family life and in some of their social and religious practices which have no longer, however, any vital meaning for them. It neither welcomes nor resists the ideas received through the new education. It dares not exert itself in the cultural sphere.

There can be no vital assimilation, in such a case, of the imposed culture. And yet the new ideas are assimilated in a fashion. They are understood and imaginatively realized; they are fixed in language and in certain imposed institutions. A drill in this language and in those institutions induces certain habits of soulless thinking which appear like real thinking. Springing as these ideas do from a rich and strong life—the life of the West—they induce in us a shadow mind that functions like a real mind except in the matter of genuine creativeness. One would have expected after a century of contact with the vivifying ideas of the West that there should be a vigorous output of Indian contribution in a distinctive Indian style to the culture and thought of the modern world,—contribution specially to the humane subjects like history, philosophy or literature, a contribution such as may be enjoyed by our countrymen who still happen to retain their vernacular mind and which might be recognized by others as reflecting the distinctive soul of India. Barring the contribution of a few men of genius,—and genius is largely independent of the times,—there is not much evidence of such creative work done by our educated men.

I may refer also to more modest forms of creativeness, creativeness such as is evidenced in the daily business of our lives, e.g., in the formation of judgments about our real position in the world. We speak of world movements and have a fair

* This discourse was given at a meeting of the students of Hooghly College of which the writer was principal, during 1928-30. The present paper was recovered from Dr. Bhattacharya's unpublished writings.

acquaintance with the principles and details of Western life and thought, but we do not always sufficiently realize where we actually stand today and how to apply our bookish principles to our situation in life. We either accept or repeat the judgments passed on us by Western culture, or we impotently resent them but have hardly any estimates of our own, wrung from an inward perception of the realities of our position.

In the field of politics, for example, we are only today beginning to realize that we have for long wrongly counted on principles that have application only to countries that are already free and already established and have not had sufficient perception of the dark thing they call 'power' which is more real than any logic or political scholarship. In the field of social reform, we have never cared to understand the inwardness of our traditional social structure and to examine how far the sociological principles of the West are universal in their application. We have contented ourselves either with an unthinking conservatism or with an imaginary progressiveness merely imitative of the West.

Then again in the field of learning, how many of us have had distinctively Indian estimates of Western literature and thought? It is possible for a foreigner to appreciated the literature of a country, but it is only to be expected that his mind would react to it differently from the mind of a native of the country. A Frenchman, for example, would not, I imagine, appreciate Shakespeare just as an Englishman would do. Our education has largely been imparted to us through English literature. The Indian mind is much further removed by tradition and history than the French or the German mind for the spirit of English literature, and yet no Indian, so far as I am aware, has passed judgments on English literature that reflect his Indian mentality.

His judgments do not differ materially from the judgment of an English critic and that raises the suspicion whether it is his judgment at all, whether it is not merely the mechanical thinking of the galvanic mind induced in us through our Western education.

In philosophy hardly anything that has been written by a modern educated Indian shows that he has achieved a synthesis of Indian thought with Western thought. There is nothing like a judgment of Western systems from the standpoint of Indian philosophy, and although some appraisement of Indian philosophy has been attempted from the Western standpoint, there appears to be no recognition yet that a criticism of the fundamental notions of either philosophy is necessary before there can be any useful comparative estimate. And yet is in philosophy that one would look for an effective contact between Eastern and Western ideas. The most prominent contribution of ancient India to the culture of the world is in the field of philosophy and if the modern Indian mind is to philosophise at all to any purpose, it has to confront Eastern thought and Western thought with one another and attempt a synthesis or a reasoned rejection of either, if that were possible. It is in philosophy, if anywhere, that the task of discovering the soul of India is imperative for the modern Indian; the task of achieving, if possible, the continuity of his old self with his present day self, of realizing what is nowadays called the Mission of India, if it has any. Genius can unveil the soul of India in art, but it is through philosophy that we can methodically attempt to discover it.

Our education has not so far helped us to understand ourselves, to understand the significance of our past, the realities of our present and our mission of the future. It has tended to drive our real mind into the unconscious and to replace it by a shadow mind that has no roots in our past and in our real present. Our old mind cannot be wholly driven underground and its imposed substitute cannot function effectively and productively. The result is that here is a confusion between the two minds and a hopeless Babel in the world of ideas. Our thought is hybrid through and through and inevitably sterile. Slavery has entered into our very soul.

The hybridization of our ideas is evidenced by the strange medley of vernacular and English in which our educated people speak to one another. For the expression of cultural ideas specially we find it very difficult to use the pure vernacular medium. If I were asked, for example, to conduct today's discourse* here in Bengali, I would have to make a particularly strenuous effort. One notices a laudable tendency at the present day to make such an effort. It is not that it is always successful. Perhaps that is only to be expected in a period of transition. If the language difficulty could be surmounted, it would mean a big step towards the achievement of what I have called Swaraj in Ideas.

The hybridization of ideas brought about by our education and the impact of Western political, social and economic institutions on our daily life is one of the most distressing features of our present situation. It is unnatural and may be regarded with the same sentiment with which an old-world Hindu looks upon varna-saṃkara. It does not simply mean a confusion in the intellectual region. All vital ideas involve ideals. They embody an entire theory and an insight into life. Thought or reason may be universal, but ideas are carved out of it differently by different cultures according to their respective genius. No idea of one cultural language can exactly be translated in another cultural language. Every culture has its distinctive 'physiognomy' which is reflected in each vital idea and ideal presented by the culture.

A patchwork of ideas of different cultures offends against scholarly sense just as much as patchwork of ideals offends against the spiritual sense. There is room indeed for an adjustment and synthesis, within limits of different cultures and cultural ideals. Life means adaptation to varying times and to varying ideals. But we are not always clear about the method of this adaptation. As we have to live, we have to accept facts and adapt our secular life and secular ideas to the times. We have to alter ourselves here to suit the situation. In spiritual life, however, there is no demand for compromising our ideals in order to have a smooth sailing with the times. Here, if possible and so far as lies in our power, the times have to be adapted to our life and not our life to the times.

But the world confronts us not only with aggressive interests but also with aggressive ideals. What response should our traditional ideals make to these imposed ideals? We may respect the new ideals without accepting them, we may attempt a synthesis without compromise or we may accept them as the fulfillment of our ideals. Different responses may be demanded with respect to different ideals, but in any case a patchwork without adjustment or with a mechanical adjustment, if complacently accepted as a solution, is an evil, as no ideal here gets the entire devotion of the soul. Where different ideals are accepted in the prayerful hope that a synthesis will come, the patchwork is not accepted as a solution and need not be an evil.

We talk—a little too glibly perhaps—of a conflict of the ideas and ideals of the West with our traditional ideas and ideals. In many cases it is a confusion rather than a conflict and the real problem is to clear up the confusion and to make it develop in the first instance into a definite conflict. The danger is in the complacent acquiescence in the confusion. The realization of a conflict of ideals implies a deepening of the soul. There is conflict proper only when one is really serious about ideals, feels each ideal to be a matter of life and death. We sometimes sentimentally indulge in the thought of a conflict before we are really serious with either ideal.

We speak also a little too readily of the demand for a synthesis of the ideals of the East and the West. It is not necessary in every case that a synthesis should be attempted. The ideals of a community spring from its past history and from the soil: they have not necessarily a universal application, and they are not always self-luminous to other communities. There are ideals of the West which we may respect from a distance without recognizing any specific appeal to ourselves. Then again there are ideals that have a partial appeal to us, because they have an affinity with our own ideals, though still with a foreign complexion. What they prescribe to us is to be worshipped in our own fashion with the ceremonials of our own religion. The form of practical life in which an ideal has to be translated, has to be decided by ourselves according to the genius of our own community. A synthesis of our ideals with western ideals is not demanded in every case. Where it is demanded, the foreign ideal is to be assimilated to our ideal and not the other way. There is no demand for the surrender of our individuality in any case: *Svadharme ndidhanam sreyah paradharmo bhayavahah.*

There are those who take this emphasis on the individuality of a historical community to be overstrained. It appears to them to be the expression of national, communal or racial conceit and the excuse for a perverse obscurantism. They believe in abstract self-luminous ideals for all humanity, in a single universal religion and a single universal reason.

There is, however, a case for universalism. The progress of a community and of humanity implies a gradual simplification and unification of ideals. This is just the rationalizing movement, the emergence of a common reason. We have to distinguish, however, between two forms of rationalism, two directions of this simplifying movement. In the one, reason is born after the travail of the spirit: rationalism is here the efflux of reverence, reverence for the traditional institutions through which customary sentiments are deepened into transparent ideals. In the other form of rationalism—what is commonly meant by the name, the simplification and generalization of ideals is effected by unregenerate understanding with its mechanical separation of the essential from the inessential. The essential is judged as such here not through reverence, not through deepened spiritual insight, but through the accidental likes and dislikes of the person judging. Customs and institutions bound up with age-long sentiments are brushed aside (in the name of reason) as meaningless and dead without any imaginative effort to realize them in an attitude of humility. Decisions as to what is essential or inessential have indeed to be taken, for time tarries not and mere historical sentimentalism will not avail. In practical life, one may have to move before ideals have clarified; but it is well to recognize the need of humility and patience in the adjustment of the world of ideas. Order is involved in the world of our ideas through infinite patience and humility. That is the right kind of rationalism: it is only in the wrong and graceless form of rationalism that brusque decisions in the practical manner are taken in the name of reason, in the world of our ideals.

There is then a legitimate and obligatory form of rationalism. It is wrong not to accept an ideal that is felt to be a simpler and deeper expression of our own ideals simply because it hails from a foreign country. To reject it would be to insist on individuality for the sake of individuality and would be a form of national conceit and obscurantism. The acceptance of such an ideal is really no surrender of individuality : to serve this foreign god is to serve our own god: the foreign ideal is here in our own ideal. The guru or teacher has to be accepted when he is found to be a real guru, whatever the community from which he comes. But it is not every foreign ideal that is felt to be the soul of our own ideal. Some foreign ideals have affinity with our own, and are really alternative expressions of them in a foreign idiom that has no sacredness for us and there are others which have no real application to our conditions.

It is sometimes forgotten by the advocates of universalism that the so-called universalism of reason or of religion is only in the making and cannot be appealed to as an actually established code of universal principles. What is universal is only the spirit, the loyalty to our own ideals and the openness to other ideals, the determination not to reject them if they are found within our ideals and not to accept them till they are so found. The only way to appraise a new ideal is to view it through our actual ideal; the only way to find a new reverence is to deepen our old reverence. Progress in the spiritual world is not achieved by a detached reason judging between an old god and a new god. The way to know facts is not the way to know values.

So much for the objection, which is often raised in the name of universalism, to the stress I have laid on the individuality of Indian thought and spirit, on the conservatism of the distinctive values evolved through ages of continuous historical life of Indian society. I have thought it necessary to examine universalism in some detail at the risk of tiring the reader with abstract arguments because this appears to me to be our greatest danger. It is the inevitable result of our 'rootless' education and it stands more than anything else in the way of what I call Swaraj in Ideas.

The other danger of national conceit and the unthinking glorification of everything in our culture and depreciation of everything in other cultures appears to me, in our circumstances, to require less stressing. Not that it is less serious abstractly considered, but as a matter of act our educated men suffer more from over-diffidence than from over-confidence, more from a 'rootless' universalism than from clinging particulars. We are more ready to accept other's judgments about us than to resent them. There is the old immemorial habit of regarding what we are taught as sacred learning, and the habit is not easily altered even though the learning imparted is the opinion of others—opinion about us, for example, of men who might be presumed to be ignorant of us and unsympathetic to us. There is so much, kind or unkind, written about us and preached to us by others that raises the legitimate question if they have a sufficient perception of the inwardness of our life. *Prima facie* it is very difficult for a foreigner to understand the mind of a people from whom he is widely removed by tradition and history unless he has intimately participated in their life for a long time. It is only natural that the people in question should receive his judgment about them with a certain amount of mental reserve. It might lead them to self-examination if the foreigner is not obviously ignorant and abusive; but docile acceptance is not certainly demanded in the first instance.

Now there is a good deal in the name of learning—history, philosophy or moral sermon—imparted to us through our education which is unconsciously or consciously of a tendentious or propagandist character. They imply a valuation of ourselves, an appraisement of our past history and present position from a foreign standard. Our attitude towards them should be one of critical reserve, and not docile acceptance. And yet the critical attitude would in many cases be condemned by our foreign teachers and by our own educated men as uncultured and almost as absurdly ignorant as a hesitation to accept the truth of geometry. That is inevitable where the education of a people is undertaken by foreign rulers. There is bound in such a case to be some imposition of foreign valuations on the learner and a discouragement of the critical attitude.

The question of imposition does not arise in the case of certain branches of learning—mathematics and the natural sciences, for example, which have no nationality and imply no valuation. Whenever there is valuation, there is the suspicion of a particular point of view—national, communal or racial, of the person who judges the value. A valuation of our culture by a foreigner from the standpoint of his own culture should be regarded by us as meant not for our immediate acceptance but for our critical examination. It should be a fillip to which we should react. I remember a remark of Sir John Woodroffe to this purpose. That our first impulse here should be one of self-defensive resentment is only natural and need not imply an uncultured self-conceit. Docile acceptance without criticism would mean slavery.

The critical attitude is demanded pre-eminently in the field of valuations of ideals. Mere acceptance here makes not only for confusion but for moral evil. But barring the concepts of sciences—even there may be some doubt—all concepts and ideals have the distinctive character of the particular culture to which they belong. What should be our reaction to such cultural ideas? They have to be accepted, but as metaphors and symbols to be translated into our own indigenous concepts. The ideas embodied in a foreign language are properly understood only when we can express them in our own way. I plead for a genuine translation of foreign ideas into our native ideas before we accept or reject them. Let us everywhere resolutely think in our own concepts. It is only thus that we can think productively on our own account.

In politics our educated men have been compelled to realize by the logic of facts that they have absolutely no power for good, though they have much power for evil, unless they can carry the masses with them. In other fields there is not sufficient realization of this circumstance. In the social sphere, for example, they still believe that they can impose certain reforms on the masses—by mere preaching from without, by passing resolutions in social conferences and by legislation. In the sphere of ideas, there is hardly yet any realization that we can think effectively only when we think in terms of the indigenous ideas that pulsate in the life and mind of the masses. We condemn the caste system of our country, but we ignore the fact that we who have received Western education constitute a caste more exclusive an intolerant than any of the traditional castes. Let us resolutely break down the barriers of the new caste, let us come back to the cultural stratum of the real Indian people and evolve a culture along with them suited to the times and to our native genius. That would be to achieve Swaraj in Ideas.

2

AN EASTERN UNIVERSITY

Rabindranath Tagore

[The western universities provide their students an opportunity to learn what the European nations have contributed to their culture. In India, however,—"there is not a single University established in the modern time where a foreign or an Indian student can properly be acquainted with the best products of the Indan mind." It is no doubt true that Tagore looks forward to intellectual and cultural cooperation between East and West. It was partly with this intention that he set up Viswa Bharati, but this cooperation will be fruitful—Tagore emphasises—only when Asia knows her mind and heritage. Only then it (Viswa Bharati) can open a new vista and not just be a pale imitation of the west. Tagore is not opposed to the assimilation of western ideas and culture; in fact, he is all for it. Only he is opposed to "the artificial arrangement by which foreign

---

*From *Selection from the Works of Rabindranath Tagore* (Macmillan and Co., Bombay, 1946).

> education tends to occupy all the space of our national mind, and thus kills, or hampers, the great oppotunity for the creation of a new thought-power by a new combination of truths."—Editor]

In the midst of much that is discouraging in the present state of the world, there is one symptom of vital promise. Asia is awakening. This great event, if it be but directed along the right lines, is full of hope, not only for Asia herself, but for the whole world.

On the other hand, it has to be admitted that the relationship of the West with the East, growing more and more complex and widespread for over two centuries, far from attaining its true fulfillment, has given rise to a universal spirit of conflict. The consequent strain and unrest have profoundly disturbed Asia, and antipathetic forces have been accumulating for years in the depth of the Eastern mind.

The meeting of the East and the West has remained incomplete, because the occasions of it have not been disinterested. The political and commercial adventures carried on by Western races—very often by force and against the interest and wishes of the countries they have dealt with—have created a moral alienation, which is deeply injurious to both parties. The perils threatened by this unnatural relationship have long been contemptuously ignored by the West. But the blind confidence of the strong in their apparent invincibility has often led them, from their dream of security, into terrible surprises of history.

It is not the fear of danger or loss to one people or another, however, which is most important. The demoralizing influence of the constant estrangement between the two hemispheres, which affects the baser passions of man,—pride, greed and hypocrisy on the one hand; fear, suspiciousness and flattery on the other,—has been developing, and threatens us with a world-wide spiritual disaster.

The time has come when we must use all our wisdom to understand the situation, and to control it, with stronger trust in moral guidance than in any array of physical forces.

In the beginning of man's history his first social object was to form a community, to grow into a people. At that early period, individuals were gathered together within geographical enclosures. But in the present age, with its facility of communication, geographical barriers have almost lost their reality, and great federation of men, which is waiting either to find its true scope or to break asunder in a final catastrophe, is not a meeting of individuals, but of various human races. Now the problem before us is of one single country, which is this earth, where the races as individuals must find both their freedom of self-expression and their bond of federation. Mankind must realize a unity, wider in range, deeper in sentiment, stronger in power than ever before. Now that the problem is large, we have to solve it on a bigger scale, to realize the God in many by a large faith and to build the temple of our faith on a sure and world-wide basis.

The first step towards realization is to create opportunities for revealing the different peoples to one another. This can never be done in those fields where the exploiting utilitarian spirit is supreme. We must find some meeting-ground, where there can be no question of conflicting interests. One of such places is the University, where we can work together in a common pursuit of truth, share together our common heritage, and realise that artists in all parts of the world have created forms of beauty, scientists discovered secrets of the universe, philosophers solved the problems of existence, saints made the truth of the spiritual world organic in their own lives, not merely for some particular race to which they belonged, but for all mankind. When the science of meteorology knows the earth's atmosphere as continuously one, affecting the different parts of the world differently, but in a harmony of adjustments, it knows and attains truth. And so, too, we must know that the great mind of man is one, working through the many differences which are needed to ensure the full result of its fundamental unity. When we understand this truth in a disinterested spirit, it teaches us to respect all the differences in man that are real, yet remain conscious of our oneness; and to know that perfection of unity is not in uniformity, but in harmony.

This is the problem of the present age. The East, for its own sake and for the sake of the world, must not remain unrevealed. The deepest source of all calamities in history is misunderstanding. For where we do not understand, we can never be just.

Being strongly impressed with the need and the responsibility, which every individual today must realise according to his power, I have formed the nucleus of an International University in India, as one of the best means of promoting mutual understanding between the East and the West. This Institution, according to the plan I have in mind, will invite students from the West to study the different systems of Indian philosophy, literature, art and music in their proper environment, encouraging them to carry on research work in collaboration with the scholars already engaged in this task.

India has her renaissance. She is preparing to make her contribution to the world of the future. In the past she produced her great culture, and in the present age she has an equally important contribution to make to the culture of the New World which is emerging from the wreckage of the Old. This is a momentous period of her history, pregnant with precious possibilities, when any disinterested offer of co-operation from any part of the West will have an immense moral value, the memory of which will become brighter as the regeneration of the East grows in vigour and creative power.

The Western Universities give their students an opportunity to learn what all the European peoples have contributed to their Western culture. Thus the intellectual mind of the West has been luminously revealed to the world. What is needed to complete this illumination is for the East to collect its own scattered lamps and offer them to the enlightenment of the world.

There was a time when the great countries of Asia had, each of them, to nurture its own civilization apart in comparative seclusion. Now has come the age of coordination and co-operation. The seedlings that were reared within narrow plots must now be transplanted into the open fields. They must pass the test of the world-market, if their maximum value is to be obtained.

But before Asia is in a position to co-operate with the culture of Europe, she must base her own structure on a synthesis of all the different cultures which she has. When, taking her stand on such a culture, she turns toward the West, she will take, with a confident sense of mental freedom, her own view of truth, from her own vantage-ground, and open a new vista of thought to the world. Otherwise, she will allow her priceless inheritance to crumble into dust, and, trying to replace it clumsily with feeble imitations of the West, make herself superfluous, cheap and ludicrous. If she thus loses her individuality and her specific power to exist, will it in the least help the rest of the world? Will not her terrible bankruptcy involve also the Western mind? If the whole world grows at last into an exaggerated West, then such an illimitable parody of the modern age will die, crushed beneath its own absurdity.

In this belief, it is my desire to extend by degrees the scope of this University on simple lines, until it comprehends the whole range of Eastern cultures—the Aryan, Semitic, Mongolian and others. Its object will be to reveal the Eastern mind to the world.

Of one thing I felt certain during my travels in Europe, that a genuine interest has been roused there in the philosophy and the arts of the East, from which the Western mind seeks fresh inspiration of truth and beauty. Once the East had her reputation of fabulous wealth, and the seekers were attracted from across the sea. Since then, the shrine of wealth has changed its site. But the East is famed also for her storage of wisdom, harvested by her patriarchs from long successive ages of spiritual endeavor. And when, as now, in the midst of the pursuit of power and wealth, there rises the cry of privation form the famished spirit of man, an opportunity is offered to the East to offer her store to those who need it.

Once upon a time we were in possession of such a thing as our own mind in India. It was living. It thought, it felt, it expressed itself. It was receptive as well as productive. That this mind could be of any use in the process, or in the end, of our education was overlooked by our modern educational dispensation. We are provided with buildings and books and other magnificent burdens calculated to suppress our mind. The latter was treated like a library-shelf solidly made of wood, to be loaded with leather-bound volumes of second-hand information. In consequence, it has lost its own colour and character, and has borrowed polish from the carpenter's shop. All this has cost us money, and also our finer ideas, while our intellectual vacancy has been crammed with what is described in official reports as Education. In fact, we have bought our spectacles at the expense of our eyesight.

In India our goddess of learning is *Saraswati*. My audience in the West, I am sure, will be glad to know that her complexion is white. But the signal fact is that she is living and she is a woman, and her seat is on a lotus-flower. The symbolic meaning of this is, that she dwells in the centre of life and the heart of all existence, which opens itself in beauty to the light of heaven.

The Western education which we have chanced to know is impersonal. Its complexion is also white, but it is the whiteness of the white-washed class-room wall. It dwells in the cold-storage compartments of lessons and the ice-packed minds of the school-masters. The effect which it had on my mind when, as a boy, I was compelled to go to school, I have described elsewhere. My feeling was very much the same as a tree might have, which was not allowed to live its full life, but was cut down to be made into packing-cases.

The introduction of this education was not a part of the solemn marriage ceremony which was to unite the minds of the East and West in mutual understanding. It represented an artificial method of training specially calculated to produce the carriers of the white man's burden. This want of ideals still clings to our education system, though our Universities have latterly burdened their syllabus with a greater number of subjects than before. But it is only like adding to the bags of wheat the bullock carries to market; it does not make the bullock any better off.

Mind, when long deprived of its natural food of truth and freedom of growth, develops and unnatural craving for success; and our students have fallen victims to the mania for success in examinations. Success consists in obtaining the largest number of marks with the strictest economy of knowledge. It is a deliberate cultivation of disloyalty to truth, of intellectual dishonesty, of a foolish imposition by which the mind is encouraged to rob itself. But as we are by means of it made to forget the existence of mind, we are supremely happy at the result. We pass examinations, and shrivel up into clerks, lawyers and police inspectors, and we die young.

Universities should never be made into mechanical organizations for collecting and distributing knowledge. Through them the people should offer their intellectual hospitality, their wealth of mind to others, and earn their proud right in return to receive gifts from the rest of the world. But in the whole length and breadth of India there is not a single University established in the modern time where a foreign or an Indian student can properly be acquainted with the best products of the Indian mind. For that we have to cross the sea, and knock at the doors of France and Germany. Educational institutions in our country are India's alms-bowl of knowledge; they lower our intellectual self-respect; they encourage us to make a foolish display of decorations composed of borrowed feathers.

This it was that led me to found a school in Bengal, in face of many difficulties and discouragements, and in spite of my own vocation as a poet, who finds his true inspiration only when he forgets that he is a schoolmaster. It is my hope that in this school a nucleus has been formed, round which an indigenous University of our own land will find its natural growth—a University which will help India's mind to concentrate and to be fully conscious of itself; free to seek the truth and make this truth its own wherever found, to judge by its own standard, give expression to its own creative genius, and offer its wisdom to the guests who come from other parts of the world.

Man's intellect has a natural pride in its own aristocracy, which is the pride of its culture. Culture only acknowledges the excellence whose criticism is in its inner perfection, not in any external success. When this pride succumbs to some compulsion of necessity or lure of material advantage, it brings humiliation to the intellectual man. Modern India, through her very education, has been made to suffer this humiliation. Once she herself provided her children with a culture which was the product of her own ages of thought and creation. But it has been thrust aside, and we are made to tread the mill of passing examinations, not for learning anything, but for notifying that we are qualified for employments under organizations conducted in English. Our educated community is not a cultured community, but a community of qualified candidates. Meanwhile the proportion of possible employments to the number of claimants had gradually been growing narrower, and the consequent disaffection has been widespread. At last the very authorities who are responsible for this are blaming their victims. Such is the perversity of human nature. It bears its worst grudge against those it has injured.

It is as if some tribe which had the primitive habit of decorating its tribal members with birds' plumage were some day to hold these very birds guilty of the crime of being extinct. There are belated attempts on the part of our governors to read us pious homilies about disinterested love of learning, while the old machinery goes on working, whose product is not education but certificates. It is good to remind the fettered bird that its wings are for soaring; but it is better to cut the chain which is holding it to its perch. The most pathetic feature of the tragedy is that the bird itself has learnt to use its chain for its ornament, simply because the chain jingles in fairly respectable English.

In the Bengali language there is a modern maxim which can be translated, "He who learns to read and write rides in a carriage and pair." In English there is a similar proverb, "Knowledge is power." It is an offer of a prospective bribe to the student, a promise of an ulterior reward which is more important than knowledge itself. Temptations, held before us a inducements to be good or to pursue uncongenial paths, are most often flimsy lies or half-truths, such as the oft-quoted maxim of respectable piety, "Honesty is the best policy," at which politicians all over the world seem to laugh in their sleeves. But unfortunately, education conducted under a special providence of purposefulness, of eating the fruit of knowledge from the wrong end, *does* lead one to that special paradise on earth, the daily rides in one's own carriage and pair. And the West, I have heard from authentic sources, is aspiring in its education after that special cultivation of worldliness.

Where society is comparatively simple and obstructions are not too numerous, we can clearly see how the life-process guides education in its vital purpose. The system of folk-education, which is indigenous to India, but is dying out, was one with the people's life. It flowed naturally through the social channels and made its way everywhere. It is a system of widespread irrigation of culture. Its teachers, specially trained men, are in constant requisition, and find crowded meetings in our villages, where they repeat the best thoughts and express the ideals of the land in the most effective form. The mode of instruction includes the recitation of epics, expounding of the scriptures, reading from the Puranas, which are the classical records of old history, performance of plays founded upon the early myths and legends, dramatic narration of the lives of ancient heroes, and the singing in chorus of songs from the old religious literature. Evidently, according to this system, the best function of education is to enable us to realise that to live as a man is great, requiring profound philosophy for its ideal, poetry for its expression, and heroism in its conduct. Owning to this vital method of culture the common people of India, though technically illiterate, have been made conscious of the sanctity of social relationships, entailing constant sacrifice and self-control, urged and supported by ideals collectively expressed in one word, *Dharma.*

Such a system of education may sound too simple for the complexities of modern life. But the fundamental principle of social life in its different stages of development remains the same; and in no circumstance can the truth be ignored that all human complexities must harmonise in organic unity with life, failing which there will be endless conflict. Most things in the civilized world occupy more than their legitimate space. Much of their burden is needless. By bearing this burden civilized man may be showing great strength, but he displays little skill. To the gods, viewing this from on high, it must seems like the flounderings of a giant who has got out of his depth and knows not how to swim.

The main source of all forms of voluntary slavery is the desire of gain. It is difficult of fight against this when modern civilization in tainted with such a universal contamination of avarice. I have realised it myself in the little boys of my own school. For the first few years there is no trouble. But as soon as the upper class is reached, their worldly wisdom—the malady of the age—begins to assert itself. They rebelliously insist that they must no longer learn, but rather pass examinations. Professions in the modern age are more numerous and lucrative than ever before. They need specialization of training and knowledge, tempting education to yield its spiritual freedom to the claims of utilitarian ambitions. But man's deeper nature is hurt; his smothered life seeks to be liberated from the suffocating folds and sensual ties of prosperity. And this is why we find almost everywhere in the world a growing dissatisfaction with the prevalent system of teaching, which betrays the encroachment of senility and worldly prudence over pure intellect.

In India, also, a vague feeling of discontent has given rise to numerous attempts at establishing national schools and colleges. But, unfortunately, our very education has been successful in depriving us of our real initiative and our courage of thought. The training we get in our schools has the constant implication in it that it is not for us to produce but to borrow. And we are casting about to borrow our educational plans from European institutions. The trampled plants of Indian corn are dreaming of recouping their harvest from the neighboring wheat fields. To change the figure, we forget that, for proficiency in walking, it is better to train the muscles of our own legs than to strut upon wooden ones of foreign make, although they clatter and cause more surprise at our skill in using them than if they were living and real.

But when we go to borrow help from a foreign neighborhood we are apt to overlook the real source of help behind all that is external and apparent. Had the deep-water fishes happened to produce a scientist who chose the jumping of a monkey for his research work, I am sure he would give most of the credit to the branches of the trees and very little to the monkey itself. In a foreign University we see the branching wilderness of its buildings, furniture, regulations, and syllabus, but the monkey, which is a difficult creature to catch and more difficult to manufacture, we are likely to treat as a mere accident of minor importance. It is convenient for us to overlook the fact that among the Europeans the living spirit of the University is widely spread in their society, their parliament, their literature, and the numerous activities of their corporate life. In all these functions they are in perpetual touch with the great personality of land which is creative and heroic in its constant acts of self-expression and self-sacrifice. They have their thoughts published in their books as well as through the medium of living men who think those thoughts, and who criticize, compare and disseminate them. Some at least of the drawbacks of their academic education are redeemed by the living energy of the intellectual personality pervading their social organism. It is like the stagnant reservoir of water which finds its purification in the showers of rain to which it keeps itself open. But, to our misfortune, we have in India all the furniture of the European University except the human teacher. We have, instead, mere purveyors of book-lore in whom the paper god of the bookshop has been made vocal.

A most important truth, which we are apt to forget, is that a teacher can never truly teach unless he is still learning himself. A lamp can never light another lamp unless it continues to burn its own flame. The teacher who has come to the end to his subject, who has no living traffic with his knowledge, but merely repeats his lessons to his students, can only load their minds; he cannot quicken them. Truth not only must inform but inspire. If the inspiration dies out, and the information only accumulates, then truth loses its infinity. The greater parts of our learning in the schools has been wasted because, for most of our teachers, their subjects are like dead specimens of once living things, with which they have a learned acquaintance, but no communication of life and love.

The educational institution, therefore, which I have in mind has primarily for its object the constant pursuit of truth, from which the imparting of truth naturally follows. It must not be a dead cage in which living minds are fed with food artificially prepared. It should be an open house, in which students and teachers are at one. They must live their complete life together, dominated by a common aspiration for truth and a need of sharing all the delights of culture. In former days the great master craftsmen had students in their workshops where they co-operated in shaping things to perfection. That was the place where knowledge could become living—that knowledge which not only has its substance and law, but its atmosphere subtly informed by a creative personality. For intellectual knowledge also has its aspect of creative art, in which the man who explores truth expresses something which is human in him—his enthusiasm, his courage, his sacrifice, his honesty, and his skill. In merely academicals teaching we find subjects, but not the man who pursues the subjects;

therefore the vital part of education remains incomplete.

For our Universities we must claim, not labeled packages of truth and authorised agents to distribute them, but truth in its living association with her lovers and seekers and discoverers. Also we must know that the concentration of the mind-forces scattered throughout the country is the most important mission of a University, which, like the nucleus of a living cell, should be the centre of the intellectual life of the people.

The bringing about of an intellectual unity in India is, I am told, difficult to the verge of impossibility owing to the fact that India has so many different languages. Such as statement is as unreasonable as to say that man, because he has a diversity of limbs, should find it impossible to realise life's unity in himself, and that only an earthworm composed of a tail and nothing else could truly know that it had a body.

Let us admit that India is not like anyone of the great countries of Europe, which has its own separate language; but is rather like Europe herself, branching out into different peoples with many different languages. And yet Europe has a common civilization, with an intellectual unity which is not based upon uniformity of language. It is true that in the earlier stages of her culture the whole of Europe had Latin for her learned tongue. That was in her intellectual budding time, when all her petals of self-expression were closed in one point. But the perfection of her mental unfolding was not represented by the singularity of her literary vehicle. When the great European countries found their individual languages, then only the true federation of culture became possible in the West, and the very differences of the channels made the commerce of ideas in Europe so richly copious and so variedly active. We can well imagine what the loss to European civilization would be if France, Italy and Germany, and England herself, had not through their separate agencies contributed to the common coffer their individual earnings.

There was a time with us when India had her common language of culture in Sanskrit. But, for the complete commerce of her thought, she required that all her vernaculars should attain their perfect powers, through which her different peoples might manifest their idiosyncrasies; and this could never be done through a foreign tongue.

In the United States, in Canada and other British Colonies, the language of the people is English. It has a great literature which had its birth and growth in the history of the British Islands. But when this language, with all its products and acquisitions, matured by ages on its own mother soil, is carried into foreign lands, which have their own separate history and their own life growth, it must constantly hamper the indigenous growth of culture and destroy individuality of judgment and the perfect freedom of self-expression. The inherited wealth of the English language, with all its splendor, becomes an impediment when taken into different surroundings, just as when lungs are given to the whale in the sea. If such is the case even with races whose grandmother-tongue naturally continues to be their own mother-tongue, one can imagine what sterility it means for a people which accepts, for its vehicle of culture, an altogether foreign language. A language is not like an umbrella or an overcoat, that can be borrowed by unconscious or deliberate mistake; it is like the living skin itself. If the body of a draught-horse enters into the skin of a race-horse, it will be safe to wager that such an anomaly will never win a race, and will fail even to drag a cart. Have we not watched some modern Japanese artists imitating European art? The imitation may sometimes produce clever results; but such cleverness has only the perfection of artificial flowers which never bear fruit.

All great countries have their vital centers for intellectual life, where a high standard of learning is maintained, where the minds of the people are naturally attracted, where the minds of the people are naturally attracted, where they find their genial atmosphere, in which to prove their worth and to contribute their share to the country's culture. Thus they kindle, on the common altar of the land, that great sacrificial fire which can radiate sacred light of wisdom abroad.

Athens was such a centre in Greece, Rome in Italy; and Paris is such today in France. Benares has been and still continues to our Sanskrit culture. But Sanskrit learning does not exhaust all the elements of culture that exist in modern India.

If we were to take for granted, what some people maintain, that Western culture is the only source of light for our mind, then it would be like depending for daybreak upon some star, which is the sun of a far distant sphere. The star may give us light, but not the day; it may give us direction in our voyage of exploration, but it can never open the full view of truth before our eyes. In fact, we can never use this cold starlight for stirring the sap in our branches, and giving colour and bloom to our life. This is the reason why European education has become for India mere school lessons and no culture; a box of matches, good for the small uses of illumination, but not the light of morning, in which the use and beauty, and all the subtle mysteries of life are blended in one.

Then, again, let us admit that modern Science is Europe's great gift to humanity for all time to come. We, in India, must claim it from her hands, and gratefully accept it in order to be saved from the curse of futility by lagging behind. We shall fail to reap the harvest of the present age if we delay.

What I object to is the artificial arrangement by which foreign education tends to occupy all the space of our national mind, and thus kills, or hampers, the great opportunity for the creation of a new thought-power by a new combination of truths. It is this which makes me urge that all the elements in our own culture have to be strengthened, not to resist the Western culture, but truly to accept and assimilate it; to use it for our sustenance, not as our burden; to get mastery over this culture, and not to live on its outskirts as the hewers of text and drawers of book learning.

The main river in Indian culture has flowed in four streams—the Vedic, the Puranic, the Buddhist, and the Jain. It has its source in the heights of the Indian consciousness. But a river, belonging to a country, is not fed by its own waters alone. The Tibetan Brahmaputra is a tributary to the Indian Ganges. Contributions have similarly found their way to India's original culture. The Muhammadan, for example, has repeatedly come into India from outside, laden with his own stores of knowledge and feeling and his wonderful religious democracy, bringing freshet after freshet to swell the current. To our music, our architecture, our pictorial art, our literature, the Muhammadans have made their permanent and precious contribution. Those who have studied the lives and writings of our medieval saints, and all the great religious movements that sprang up in the time of the Muhammadan rule, know how deep is our debt to this foreign current that has so intimately mingled with our life.

So, in our centre of Indian learning, we must provide for the co-ordinate study of all these different cultures—the Vedic, the Puranic, the Buddhist, the Jain, the Islamic, the Sikh and the Zoroastrian. The Chinese, Japanese, and Tibetan will also have to be added for, in the past, India did not remain isolated within her own boundaries. Therefore, in order to learn what she was, in her relation to the whole continent of Asia, these cultures too must be studied. Side by side with them must finally be placed the Western culture. For only then shall we be able to assimilate this last contribution to our common stock. A river flowing within banks is truly our own, and it can contain its due tributaries; but our relations with a flood can only prove disastrous.

There are some who are exclusively modern, who believe that the past is the bankrupt time, leaving no assets for us, but only a legacy of debts. They refuse to believe that the army which is marching forward can be fed from the rear. It is well to remind such persons that the great ages of renaissance in history were those when man suddenly discovered the seeds of thought in the granary of the past.

The unfortunate people who have lost the harvest of their past have lost their present age. They have missed their seed for cultivation, and go begging for their bare livelihood. We must not imagine that we are one of these disinherited peoples of the world. The time has come for us to break open the treasure-trove of our ancestors, and use it for our commerce of life.

Let us, with its help, make our future our own, and not continue our existence as the eternal rag pickers in other people's dustbins.

So far I have dwelt only upon the intellectual aspect of Education. For, even in the West, it is the intellectual training which receives almost exclusive emphasis. The Western universities have not yet truly recognized that fullness of expression is fullness of life. And a large part of man can never find its expression in the mere language of words. It must therefore seek for its other languages—lines and colours, sounds and movements. Through our mastery of these we not only make our whole nature articulate, but also understand man in all its attempts to reveal his innermost being in every age and clime. The great use of Education is not merely to collect facts, but to know man and to make oneself known to man. It is the duty of every human being to master, at least to some extent, not only the language of intellect, but also that personality which is the language of Art. It is a great world of reality for man—vast and profound—this growing world of his own creative nature. This is the world of Art. To be brought up in ignorance of it is to be deprived of the knowledge and use of that great inheritance of humanity, which has been growing and waiting for every one of us from the beginning of our history. It is to remain deaf to the eternal voice of Man, that speaks to all men the message that are beyond speech. From the educational point of view we know

Europe where it is scientific, or at best literary. So our notion of its modern culture is limited within the boundary lines of grammar and the laboratory. We almost completely ignore the aesthetic life of man, leaving it uncultivated, allowing weeds to grow there. Our newspapers are prolific, our meeting-places are vociferous; and in them we wear to shreds the things we have borrowed from our English teachers. We make the air dismal and damp with the tears of our grievances. But where are our arts, which, like the outbreak of spring flowers, are the spontaneous overflow of our deeper nature and spiritual magnificence?

Through this great deficiency of our modern education, we are condemned to carry to the end a dead load of dumb wisdom. Like miserable outcasts, we are deprived of our place in the festival of culture, and wait at the outer court, where the colours are not for us, nor the forms of delight, nor the songs. Ours is the education of a prison-house, with hard labour and with a drab dress cut to the limits of minimum decency and necessity. We are made to forget that the perfection of colour and form and expression belongs to the perfection of vitality—that the joy of life is only the other side of the strength of life. The timber merchant may think that the flowers and foliage are mere frivolous decorations of a tree; but if these are suppressed, he will know to his cost that the timber too will fail.

During the Mughal period, music and art in India found a great impetus from the rulers, because their whole life—not merely their official life—was lived in this land; and it is the wholeness of life from which originates Art. But our English teachers are birds of passage; they Cackle to us, but do not sing—their heart is not in the land of their exile.

Constriction of life, owing to this narrowness of culture, must no longer be encouraged. In the centre of Indian culture which I am proposing, music and art must have their prominent seat of honour, and not be given merely a tolerant nod of recognition. The different systems of music and different schools of art which be scattered in different ages and provinces of India and in the different strata of society, and also those belonging to the other great countries of Asia, which had communication with India, have to be brought there together and studied.

I have already hinted that Education should not be dragged out of its native element, the life-current of the people. Economic life covers the whole width of the fundamental basis of society because its necessities are the simplest and the most universal. Educational institutions, in order to obtain their fullness of truth, must have close association with this economic life. The highest mission of education is to help us to realise the inner principle of the unity of all knowledge and all the activities of our social and spiritual being. Society in its early stage was held together by its economic co-operation, when all its members felt in unison a natural interest in their right to live. Civilization could never have been started at all if such was not the case. And civilization will fall to pieces if it never again realises the spirit of mutual help and the common sharing of benefits in the elemental necessaries of life. The idea of such economic co-operation should be made the basis of our University. It must not only instruct, but live; not only think, but produce.

Our ancient *tapovanas,* or forest schools, which were our natural universities, were not shut off from the daily life of the people. Masters and students gathered fruit and fuel, and took their cattle out to graze, supporting themselves by the work of their own hands. Spiritual education was a part of the spiritual life itself, which comprehended all life. Our centre of culture should not only be the centre of the intellectual life of India, but the centre of her economic life also. It must co-operate with the villages round it, cultivate land, breed cattle, spin cloths, press oil from oil-seeds; it must produce all the necessaries, devising the best means, using the best materials, and calling science to its aid. Its very existence should depend upon the success of its industrial activities carried out on the co-operative principle. Which will unite the teachers and students and villagers of the neighborhood in a living and active bond of necessity. This will give us also a practical industrial training, whose motive force is not the greed of profit.

Before I conclude my paper, a delicate question remains to be considered. What must be the religious ideal that is to rule our centre of Indian culture? The one abiding ideal in the religious life of India has been *Mukti,* the deliverance of man's soul from the grip of self, its communion with the Infinite Soul through its union in *ananda* with the universe. This religion of spiritual harmony is not the logical doctrine to be taught, as a subject in the class, for half an hour each day. It is the spiritual truth and beauty of our attitude towards our surroundings, our conscious relationship with the Infinite, and the lasting power of the Eternal in the passing moments of our life. Such a religious ideal can only be made possible by making provision for students to live in intimate touch with nature, daily to grow in an atmosphere of service offered to all creatures, tending trees, feeding birds and animals, learning to feel the immense mystery of the soil and water and air.

Along with this, there should be some common sharing of life with the tillers of the soil and the humble workers in the neighboring villages; studying their crafts, inviting them to the feasts, joining them in works of co-operation for communal welfare; and in our intercourse we should be guided, not by moral maxims or the condescension of social superiority, but by natural sympathy of life for life, and by the sheer necessity of love's sacrifice for its own sake. In such an atmosphere students would learn to understand that humanity is a divine harp of many strings, waiting for its one grand music. Those who realise this unity are made ready for the pilgrimage through the night of suffering, and along the path of sacrifice, to the great meeting of Man in the future, for which the call comes to us across the darkness.

Life, in such a centre, should be simple and clean. We should never believe that simplicity of life might make us unsuited to the requirements of the society of our time. It is the simplicity of the tuning-fork, which is needed all the more because of the intricacy of strings in the instrument. In the morning of our career our nature needs the pure and the perfect note of a spiritual ideal in order to fit us for the complications of our later years.

In other words, this institution should be a perpetual creation by the co-operative enthusiasm of teachers and students, growing with the growth of their soul; a world in itself, self-sustained, independent, rich with ever renewing life, radiating life across space and time, attracting and maintaining round it a planetary system of dependent bodies. Its aim should lie in imparting life-breath to the complete man, who is intellectual as well as economic, bound by social bonds, but aspiring towards spiritual freedom and final perfection.

3

ENCOUNTERS BETWEEN CIVILIZATIONS : THE QUESTION OF THE CENTRE AND THE PERIPHERY*

Daya Krishna

[Most intellectuals of the nonwestern world subscribe to the belief that they belong to the periphery, that the centre of knowledge lies somewhere else, say at Harvard or Cambridge or Oxford. It is because this belief is deeply ingrained in their psyche that they feel "embarassed" about their not knowing even a secondrate western thinker while their counterparts in the west aren't bothered about even the finest thinkers of the East. However, there are areas of creatvity like music and dance where we don't seek outside recognition or approval. We ae convinced of the greatness of a musician like AmirKhan and a dancer like Kelucharan Mahapatra and don't seek the approval

---

*Text of the Second Fulbright Memorial Lecture delivered at Calcutta. Reproduced from *New Quest* (125, Sept.-Oct. 1997).

of the west. Daya Krishna pleads that we must give up thinking in terms of the centre and the periphery, for "there can be no such thing as fixed centres for all times" and even in the natural sciences "the centre of the cognitive enterprise has shifted from Germany and France and England to America." —Editor]

It is always a pleasure to be in Calcutta because, I have been associated with this city and its intellectual life since 1961, And "What a city"! Every time I come here it fills me with joy and pleasure. I meet old friends and make new ones. It is a city vibrant and intellectually alive. I sometimes wish that the Calcutta people were a bit more self-conscious of their achievements, their past and future though this is not the occasion to talk about it.

Today, friends, I want to talk to you about something which I am afraid very few people in India are even vaguely or marginally aware of, that is, the issue relating to what may be called "Encounters between Civilizations". In fact, the issue concerns civilizations themselves. Some of you, I am sure, would recall those days when any discussion about civilizations was not academically fashionable. Those were the days when people used to talk about civilization, mostly, of course, in terms of the West. There was a book which was quite well known at one time and discussed by many people in this country.

It was written by Clive Bell and published in the Popular Pelican Series entitled *Civilization.* I wonder how many of you would recall it today. There was, of course, the massive study of history by Toynbee who classified all known civilizations and formulated his own theory regarding the origin, growth and decline of most of them. However, gradually the study of civilizations faded from the historian's horizon and only micro-history dominated his concerns. But recently there has one again been a return to a concern with civilizations in a guise and a garb which I think is dangerous. I do not know how many of you are aware of an article that appeared in *Foreign Affairs* some time at the end of 1993. This was written by a well known political scientist, Samuel P. Huntington, who had earlier written a well-known book entitled *Political Order and Political Decay.* In fact, it was an accidental encounter with this book that led me to write a full-length work entitled *Political Development: A Critical Perspective.* This article that he wrote in *Foreign Affairs* was titled "The Clash Between Civilizations." After about a year later the *London Economist* published an editorial entitled "The International Order" which was even more disturbing to me. There had been a debate on the *Foreign Affairs* article in *Foreign Affairs* itself but even after that debate this editorial appeared in London and I will just give you a brief summary or an idea of what it contained. May I remind you of the historical situation in which these two pieces were written. The Soviet Union had collapsed, and the Cold

War had ended with the complete victory of the western world. One would naturally expect that this would be the time for the western intellectual to relax and feel "safe" in the world. But this did not happen. The article opens almost with a dream-like reality as if we were in a situation of war, sitting in a trench, where one does not know what is happening around one. The article begins with an analysis of NATO and slogans for war, analyzing the situation we are in, what we want to achieve and how we should go about achieving it.

Imagine a western intellectual talking about a clash of civilizations at a time when the western civilization had triumphed almost completely and had hardly any rival left in the world. Imagine one of the most prestigious journals of England talking of a war-like situation between civilizations! What could be more disturbing than this? In fact, if one goes through the works of western intellectuals, one is surprised at their "parochiality"; they have so deeply identified themselves with western civilization and its fortunes that they have even begun to warn their own colleagues and friends that their future is bound with the future of western civilization and that western civilization is in danger. Imagine this perception when the factual situation as it obtains is that it is the non-western civilizations which are endangered by the West.

In fact, all non-western civilizations have been put on the defensive for at least the last 300 years, if not more, and the West is today both politically and economically dominant all over the globe. There is no doubt that it uses the mechanics of the United Nations for the achievement of its own ends. Huntington has just brought out a book entitled *The New World Order* which was reviewed in the *New York Review of Books* recently. While there is an emerging global situation in which we talk of global culture and civilization, it is clear that the intellectuals of the West are unable to cope with the real universality of the situation.

I would not like to enlarge upon the challenge to the non-western intellectual which the situation poses, but at least one thing is clear to me that unless intellectuals in the non-western world, including those in India, become aware of this situation and respond to it, things are going to get worse as the emerging world will then be completely shaped by the western perception of what the global situation ought to be.

Let me return to the theme of this lecture. During the last four years, by accident, I have been interested in history. Most of you know about Professor D.P. Chattopadhyaya's project on the History of Science, Technology, Philosophy and Culture of India. This had led me gradually into the question of what civilization is a specifically what exactly has been the enterprise of the Indian Civilization in its millennia long past. What has it been seeking for the last 5000 years? In fact, I gave a lecture recently in Delhi entitled "India's Civilizational Enterprises in the third Millennium A.D.: Maintenance, Renewal and new Directions." The moment one becomes aware of the civilization's enterprises in the long millennial past, one realizes that it has also a long millennial destiny in the future that is still to unfold in time. The little span of a few centuries then ceases to matter. What one reads in the papers in the morning does not matter when one sees it in terms of the great civilizational enterprise into which the civilization enterprise into which the civilization entered sometime in 3000 or 2500 B.C., depending upon the date of the Harappan civilization.

However, what we are generally aware of is not this long enduring quest of a civilization, but only of little bits of it that occur in the present that we accidentally happen to occupy. But we do not realize that to live in the perceptual reality of the present is to live in a total abstraction. It is true that we act in the present but unless that action is informed not merely by the exigencies of the perceptual present, and by the awareness of the past penetrating deeply into the consciousness of the present and shaping its direction of the future, it is bound to be accidental and marginal in character.

Civilizations are the most complex creation of man, and yet the methodology of understanding them does not exist. All cognitive enterprises are confined to the specificity of the field which they have demarcated for themselves. But to see a civilizational enterprise in its totality and to try to understand it is an entirely different task altogether.

To return to the theme I began with, what we call power and wealth, economics and politics, are irrelevant to the enterprises of a civilization. It is an illusion that is engendered by those who occupy seats of political and economic power, that they are the centre, that they determine the unfoldment or reality. The civilizational reality does not cease to unfold as political centers shift and vast changes take place, or trade routes change, as wealth accumulates here and disappears after a certain time, and as cities grow and decline. This is not where the heart of a civilization lies. This is the one lesson one learns when one goes back to the understanding of the enterprises of a civilization. Where was the Mauryan Empire? Where were the Guptas? This story of centers of economic wealth is a story where new centers in place of old have always arisen and flourished for a time and then disappeared.

I want to suggest therefore, that to understand civilizations is to move one's attention away from power and wealth or from polity and economy. But where does one move it to? It is one of the perennial dilemmas in thought and action that in the present the persons who matter are only those who wield power or have wealth because they command resources, or give patronage, and because they are at the centers of the causal manipulation of things. Hence, we tend to think that they are the most important; but the movement they disappear from the scene, what remains? Only the chronicles. What begins to dominate one's attention is not the politician or even the statesman, the men of wealth are hardly remembered and if they are remembered at all, they are only remembered because they were connected with some great spiritual or intellectual movement. I think this is an important point because when the political and economic centers cease to occupy one's attention, what comes into focus are those who have contributed to or have pursued some other values such as those of knowledge or spirit or beauty in the realms of thought, religion or art. When one thinks of the past, what dominates our minds is a Plato, or a Socrates or an Aristotle, or the hundreds of persons in India such as the Buddha and Mahavira. It is seldom persons who had political power or wealth that we remember.

The western thinker today has an obsessive concern with power and wealth which has blinded him to civilizational concerns. If you accept my thesis, even provisionally, you may legitimately ask how there could be a clash between civilizations in such a perspective. The very notion of a clash between civilizations seems a contradiction in terms. There is an encounter between civilizations, yes, but a clash between civilizations? Clashes are in the realm of military encounters or in the field of trade. Sometimes we are told that clashes occur because of religion; there have been religious wars, but there have seldom been wars in the realm of knowledge or in seeking for knowledge.

So the first point that I would like to make today is that thinking about civilizations and civilizational encounters has to be disengaged, has to be completely separated from considerations of military and economic encounters. If this is accepted, then I will suggest a new direction for thinking about civilizations. A civilization that looks at its past is stuck in what may be called concern with the past. It is stuck by the achievements of the past great persons; we may have a Plato or an Aristotle, a Kant or a Hegel, or we may have a Shankar or a Ramanuja or a Gangesh; for example, one may continuously return to the task of understanding and perpetuating their thought as if they had achieved a finality in the philosophical enterprise of a civilization. Or, a civilization may consider itself to be paradigmatically represented by a Buddha, a Mahavira or a Gandhi or a Vivekanand or an Aurobindo. But we are stuck at the points which these names represent because we have forgotten to see the civilizational enterprise as an enterprise in which the Buddha and the Mahavira were merely what may be called stopping places or markers in the march of civilization in an enterprise which was unfolding. The whole panorama begins to take a new shape and a new meaning in one's consciousness the moment one sees it as a process, a process of seeking something which may be termed as the *purushartha* of a civilization. But, what is the *purushartha* of a civilization is never clear as it is unfolded gradually by a series of successive generations of masters who appear on the scene. If civilizations are seen in this way, then the encounter between them will be of a different order. It will be an encounter between the *purusharthas* of civilizations, between the *shastras* of civilizations. What is the relation between a *purushartha* and a *shastra?* I think a *shastra* gives a static form to a dynamic scene; in a sense, it is an 'enemy' of the *purushartha.*

Take Gautama, for example; he wrote the *Nyaya Sutra* and we are stuck with it. Then some one writes a *bhashya* on it and so on. Thus even though thinking itself is an infinite process it does not appear to be so to one who is stuck in the thought of the past thinkers of civilization. Similarly the realization of a *purushartha* is an infinite seeking. But when it takes the form of a *shastra,* it seems to have a finality in it like the way Aristotle was at one time seen in western civilization and from which it took almost a millennium for it to free itself. We in India, however have never consciously tried to free ourselves from the past as the West has done. On the contrary, we have tried to retain and accept every past master as a 'God' to be worshipped, cherished and imitated as far as possible. This itself may be seen in a different way as some sort of a double process in the movement of our civilization. This double process consists firstly in the attempt to build a continuum. We have to build at every step on what has gone before. There is also a necessity, to take stock of what has happened before taking the next step and moving once again. Now this is a double movement which consists of seemingly static points, a staying for a little while, and then, moving again. But if we see the succession of *shastras* in this way, we will see them as steps in a movement, seemingly static steps in a dynamic motion. Once we begin to see civilizations in this manner, then the question arises as to how we shall conceive of and understand the encounters between civilizations.

Some of you may recall Edward Shils; he was a good friend of many of us. He tried to answer this question in a certain way and that may provide a point of departure for our thought in this connection. He had come to India and after his visit wrote a book entitled *Between Tradition and Modernity: The Case of the Indian Intellectual.* Shils did not know at that time that modernity itself would be in question and that the post-modernist would appear on the scene and the whole notion of modernity itself would be seen as *passe,* something that was already over. He had talked about the question of the centre and the periphery. Not only he, almost all western intellectuals have returned to the theme again and again, assuming that they are in the centre and the rest of the world at the periphery. The whole idea of what is called colonial intellectuals, colonial arts, all the usual terms that one uses, presuppose that there is a centre and there is a periphery. In fact, the whole mentality of being on the periphery has so deeply become a part of the psyche of may intellectuals of the non-western world, that they think that the centre of knowledge lies somewhere else, at Harvard or Cambridge or Oxford of Paris. It is not in Calcutta; it is not in Delhi, it is nowhere in the non-western world. Surprisingly, even the Japanese do not see themselves as being in the centre, even thought they are "developed" by all western standards. To give you one example, I received a magazine from Japan that was published in English. I felt excited; I said, let me find out what the Japanese intellectuals are thinking. I opened it and read the editorial. You can imagine my shock when I found that the editor was complaining that the Japanese intellectuals did not know anything about Foucault. Imagine a country which is economically so powerful, technologically so advanced and innovative and its intellectuals complain that people there did not know about Foucault. Why should they know about Foucault? Nobody in Paris of France or England or America or Germany ever complains that their philosophers do not know about K.C. Bhattacharya. Why not? Can you imagine that even when one of their not very great philosophers, but a good philosopher from Columbia University, Arthur Dento, referred to K.C. Bhattacharya as a philosopher of world class, little known outside his country, no one bothered to read K.C. Bhattacharya! K.C. Bhattacharya is, of course, only a symbol, an example. The point is that no western intellectual ever feels "embarrassed" about not "knowing" about any thinker, any intellectual of the non-western world, however great he may be; while on the other hand, people in the non-western world are always "embarrassed" if some one points out their ignorance of a second-rate thinker of the western world. This is because we have accepted the notion of a centre and the periphery in our soul, in our minds. But there are exceptions. I want you to think about the reason as to why there are exceptions. Supposing I ask each one of you what ghreat, spiritual personality has been produced in West in the last four hundred years? Can you give me a name? you are not embarrassed about not knowing it, because you are quite confident that the norms and the standards for judging what a spiritual personality consists in are located in our own tradition. We have had not one, not two, not three, not four, but at least a dozen outstanding spiritual personalities in this country within the last one hundred and fifty years. Is it not amazing that India has creativity in certain fields where it does not look outside for recognition? This means that there is a centre within this civilization which the persons in the civilization accept. In such an area they do not look outward for recognition. But this is not the only area where we unquestioningly accept that the centre lies here and not elsewhere. Take music for example. This is the city where Amir Khan, a great vocalist, and innovator, and a master died in an accident. Did we ever go to the West to discover whether Amir Khan was a great singer or not? Does anybody go and ask for the western recognition of Kelucharan Mahapatra, the great dancer? I am sure most of you must have seen his dance, those of you who have not, should. When I first saw him, I found it an experience which I can never forget. He was dancing with a young, beautiful girl, his student, Madhavi Mudgal. Though he was above sixty with wrinkles on his face and she was a young, beautiful girl, no one could take their eyes off of him. That is art; that is genius.

The point is that in music and dance and spirituality we have our own standards. We do not need certificates from outside. We tend to use the term "classical" in the realm of music and dance but even the term classical has different meanings when used for different arts in the western tradition. In sculpture, for example, it usually connotes what was created in Greece, but in music and dance where does it start? It does not start from Greece. In which century were Bach or Beethovan or Mozart? As for classical ballet, when does it start? Classical western dance does not start from Greece or Rome or the Middle Ages. The term "classical" therefore does not mean the same in the context of all the realms of creativity. While in India we still have a tradition of music and dance which is continuous with the past tradition. In the fields of painting, architecture and sculpture, there seems to be no such continuity. Here we have become part of a global tradition and have no standards with which to judge our creative productions in these domains, and hence inevitably have to import those standards by which we may judge our own work.

The situation, as we said earlier, is radically different in the fields of music and dance. As for spirituality, the creativity and continuity in the tradition seems so alive that it has even become an export item in our culture because of its demand in the West. Transcendental meditation has been made a credit course of American campuses. The Hare Krishna movement of Swami Bhakti Vedantanand has made people dance on the streets of New York, London, Paris and Moscow. It has made them shave their heads and turn vegetarians. The traditions of India's spiritual seeking go back to the earliest times of which we do not have any record and this may be one of the reasons why in the field of matters relating to spiritual seeking, we still enjoy an autonomy which is unrivalled. It has not generally been noticed that spiritual seeking in India has been independent of any dogmatic theological or metaphysical belief and, unlike other religions, God has played a very insignificant role at least in the beginnings of that tradition. In the field of music and dance, there is, perhaps, a similar story though with obvious differences. The tradition of reflection on music and dance go back to the earliest Vedic times when both *Sama* and *Gandharva* were not only objects of cultivation but also theoretical reflection. In this connection Dr Mukund Lath has drawn my attention to a story that occurs in one of the earliest *brahmana* texts and I cannot resist the temptation of repeating it to you. The story is of the battle between *Suras* and *Asuras* in which the *Suras* were always defeated and died. They went to Brahma who told them to go and sing *Sama* but still they did not win and were again defeated in battle. They went once more to Brahma and complained to him about the fact that inspite of singing *Sama* they had not won the battle; then Brahma said to them "Look you have been singing *Rig* and not pure *Sama,* for pure music is without words and unless you throw the words away, you cannot have pure *Sama"*. This is of course all *Arthavada.* What the story conveys is that pure music is just *alap* with no words whosoever.

As for dance, the earliest analysis is by Tandu. It is again told in the form of a beautiful story. When Bharata had completed his treatise on *Natya* he went to Shiva and showed him the text and asked, if there was anything wrong with it. The Lord said everything is alright except that you have not included dance in it. But as he did not know much about dance he asked Tandu to find out about it and Tandu went to Shiva to see him perform so that he may understand what it consisted of. He saw Shiva dancing and analyzed his dance into its basic elements the combination of which resulted in the different dances that Shiva performed for him. Imagine a tradition where the God himself dances and where even the words of the Vedic hymns are discarded to achieve pure music. It is due to such foundational reflection where pure music and pure dance occupied the attention of those who reflected on the arts in the tradition that perhaps we still enjoy a civilizational autonomy in these areas as we do in the tradition of spiritual seeking. But while the practice in all these fields continues to be autonomous, the intellectual reflection on them can hardly be considered to be so. Our current habits of intellectual reflection have, in fact, an intrinsically ambivalent and ambiguous character as they derive from two different traditions which a have only a marginal interaction between them. In the field of philosophy, for example, most of us are rooted primarily in the western tradition. We have been trained in western philosophy right from Descartes, to Kant and Hegel to the modern period and we have also a sneaking suspicion that there may be something in Indian philosophy, thought we have only a vague acquaintance with it. But we are rooted in neither. We are like amphibious creatures between two intellectual traditions of philosophizing. Even people like K.C. Bhattacharya have been writing in English though they are rooted in their tradition. They are in both traditions and thinking creatively. On the other hand, there are pure Sanskritists who still philosophize in the older traditions they have inherited and in which they have been trained. In this very city of Calcutta, for example, there was a scholar called Anantkrishna Shastri who wrote a reply to a text which was written in the fourteenth century. He wrote a book published from Calcutta entitled *Shatbhusani* which was a reply to Vedanta Desika's well-known attack on *Advaita* which he titled *Shatbhusani.* He also replied to another work written in the fourteenth century by Jayatirtha in the Madhva School entitled *Nyayasudha* and called it *Advaitatattavasudha.* Thus the *Dvaita* and the *Visitadvaita* thinkers for the fourteenth century were sufficiently alive to be given an answer to the criticism that they had made of the *Advaita* position. But it is not that he only lived in the past. He was also sufficiently aware of the work of his contemporaries such as Vasudeva Sastri Abhayankar to whose work *Advaitamoda* he replied in his work *Advaitatattvashuddhi.* Thus in the pure Sanskrit tradition of philosophizing, there has been creative originality. There has also been creative originality among thinkers who belong to both the traditions who have written during the last, say, sixty years and have contributed something really worthwhile.

However, while in music, dance and spirituality, it is not only the centre which is in India, but also our mode of apprehending and judging them are completely internal. But, this is not true of our intellectual enterprises including even those in the field of philosophy where we had a very strong internal tradition going back to more than two millennia of recorded history. This has happened perhaps because as far as the intellectual traditions are concerned, most of us are more rooted in the western traditions of knowledge in these domains and think primarily in the context of the traditions as they developed there. To give but one example form the field of philosophy, we may take the case of K.C. Bhattacharya whom I have mentioned before. We all know that he was a great thinker, at least everybody in India accepts this. But somehow our response to him even when we accept his greatness is radically different than say, to Bhimsen Joshi. Where does this difference lie? I suggest that the difference arises from the fact that in the field of philosophy my sensibility is shaped by my acquaintance with the long philosophical tradition of the west from Plato right upto modern times. I philosophically live in this world and feel myself intellectually to be a part of it. On the contrary, the vast, complex and varied tradition of western music is mostly something "external" to me, even though I may have enjoyed occasionally some great pieces of it now and then. But it has not shaped my musical sensibility in any profound way and hence when I listen to Bhimsen Joshi my response happens to be radically different from the one I make to K.C. Bhattacharya. In the field of music and dance the student carries the creativity of the master forward. Why does this not happen in the field of philosophy? It can, and it should and the only way it can be done is to immerse ourselves once again in the philosophical issues and questions that engaged the attention of thinkers in the past and the present. In fact our deep acquaintance with intellectual traditions of India and West should help us in "freeing" ourselves from the stereotyped movements of thought in both the traditions in order to strike out in new directions.

To return to the theme of the "Encounter between Civilizations, the question of the Centre and the Periphery", I want to make a few points before I close. Firstly, encounters between civilization have occurred in the past. They occur all the time. What a civilization takes from other civilizations depends on its own weaknesses and strengths. In what field does it feel sure of itself? In what field does it create? It can borrow; it can assimilate; it can modify; it can reject. The situation changes when the encounter between civilization occurs in the context of a military imbalance. Take for instance, the whole story of the encounter between the Indian civilization and the Islamic civilization during the middle ages. Why is it, for example, that in the field of philosophy in India, there is no influence at all of Islamic philosophy? There was, at least in the north, a continuous Islamic rule of three to four hundred years and yet there is no influence of it on the philosophical thought of this country. If one reads only the Sanskrit texts of those times one would not know that there was such a thing as an Islamic political rule in this country. There was an influence in medicine, in astronomy, some in mathematics, but not in the field of philosophy.

In contrast with this, in our encounter with the West the situation just seems the opposite. There is hardly any field of knowledge which is untouched by western influence. One reason for this is that the West is cognitively dynamic in almost all fields of study. The creativity of the West in the field of the natural sciences is absolutely undeniable and it would be foolish to think that we can go back to the past traditions in these fields in our country. But it need not be so in the Social Sciences and Humanities. The Social Sciences are not so objectively scientific as is generally claimed. The Humanities, of course, are more culture-specific than even the social sciences. In these fields we can take hold of the conceptual structures of the past intellectual traditions as they evolve in the encounters with different civilizations and develop them further in the contemporary context.

We have already seen that the realms of power and wealth are irrelevant to the enterprises of a civilization, except indirectly. They can corrupt. Normally one talks only of power in this connection but wealth is as much corrupting as power, though people have hardly talked of it in this way. They both give patronage; they can foster certain things, hinder certain other things, but these are passing phenomena in the context of the millennial enterprise of a civilization. Once our attention shifts from the centers of political and economic power where does it rest? It rests on centers of cognitive, spiritual and artistic creativity. Only in the cognitive domain can a strict claim be made for objectivity and universality. In the field of arts and spirituality, diversity is the heart of the matter. Plurality is not merely encouraged but valued. A person who repeats what the master did is no artist at all. And even in the realm of philosophy if one only repeats what the masters did or the great thinkers said, one is no philosopher. Even in the sciences where there is objectivity and universality, one must move forward and point out the imperfections, or the mistakes of earlier scientists, or move to a new field of enquiry.

Now, if we see the cognitive enterprises in this way, there can be no such thing as fixed centres for all times. Take for example, the West itself. Political power has shifted from Europe to America. Even in the field of knowledge, you can see the shift within the last fifty years. It is amazing how the centre of the cognitive enterprise even in the natural sciences has shifted from Germany and France and England to America, or to people who are located in America. So, the centres even within one's civilization do not remain static.

I would suggest therefore, that we must give up thinking in terms of the centre and the periphery. There are no centres, but there are different centres in diverse fields. In certain fields, centres continue to be in the civilization where they occurred or arose in the first place. Take for example, flower arrangement in Japan or the Japanese garden. Where is the centre for the Japanese garden? The West had copied the Japanese garden but the centre of creativity within that domain still lies in the Japan. Others merely copy what happens there. Similarly, there are certain domains in which the centre still lies within India, not outside and where others copy what we do. They are other fields where the situation is ambiguous, like philosophy. In some other fields the situation is unambiguous. There is no harm in the centre being outside provided that we see that this centre is not going to be permanently outside.

In conclusion, I would say that though the intellectual in the West is parochial, we ourselves should not develop a parochial intellect. We should try to build a transcivilizational intellect or consciousness which values its own enterprises and takes from others what it considers worthwhile and assimilates it and gives it a form which is specifically its own.

I think this is one of the greatest challenges today. We stand at a point in the history of civilizations where the centres of economy and power are distorting the encounter between civilizations. Imagine what a beautiful thing it would be if all of us learn from each other and build something new on the foundations of all the civilizations that man has created until now. Yet, at this very moment when such a challenging opportunity has arisen, the western intellect has unfortunately receded and begun to see itself not only in strictly western terms but also as threatened from all non-western civilizations. Huntington is not an isolated example.

There are hundreds of others who identify themselves with West and see themselves primarily in "western" terms. For them "The West is the best and they always talk in terms of the West versus the rest". Even such intellectual giants as Husser and Heidegger share this view and see the future of civilization as bound with the fortunes of their own. We cannot have a new world civilization with such small intellects. But is a trans civilizational enterprise possible? Is a world civilization possible? I do no know because we are all shaped and structured by our own civilizations. But still it is a challenge to all of us so that a better future may possibly be built as a result not of a clash of civilizations but of a common enterprise of all civilizations in such way that each preserves its own identity without endangering the new civilization that is still to emerge in the future.

4

INDIGENIZATION OF THE SOCIAL SCIENCES*

S.C. Dube

[Dube points out that even after independence the social scientists in the former colonies retained their links with prestigious centers of learning in the west and maintained their attitude of difference, dependency and servility. As a result, there was a race to keep up with the latest trends in the west, and conceptual frameworks and methods of research were borrowed from the west. Little thought was given to their relevance to the indigenous culture. Also, the social scientists of the less developed countries wrote in a language-English in our country-whose reach was very limited. Then they published in international journals

*From *S.C. Dube on Crisis and Commitment in Social Sciences*, ed. Yogesh Atal (Abhinav, N. Delhi, 1983).

whose interests and foci were those of the affluent and advanced western countries, and of little relevance to our culture. The author pleads that social scientists in India and other less developed countries need to indigenize, that is, to relate more meaningfully to their own culture and tradition and corpus of indigenous through." Otherwise our scholarship will remain a pathetic imitation of the west and our social anthropologists will continue to commit such follies as rejecting tradition and history only because Malinowski emphasised the a-historical character of the discipline and return to them only when Louis Dumont pleaded for it. —Editor.

The Social sciences, as we know them today, are largely of Western origin. In the Third World they were a colonial import; even today they do not appear to have gained firm roots in the soil and are not adequately adapted to the social environment of their new habitat. Non-western civilizations had their own traditions of social thought and many of them even made limited use of the empirical method for understanding their societies, but such intellectual quests did not crystallize sufficiently to acquire disciplinary individuality. In these civilizations speculation and reflection concerning man and society gained greater strength in the direction of social ethics and philosophy; there was much less emphasis on exploration of the existential reality. The form in which the social sciences have developed in the societies of the Third World are unmistakably shaped by the Western intellectual impact.

The different disciplines under the rubric of the social sciences was conditioned by the milieu in which they originated. Most of the pioneering studies were culture-specific and represented the response of perceptive and creative minds to the social reality they encountered. With exception of anthropology, which studied exotic cultures, in all other social sciences the earlier studies were done within the societies of pioneers. Analytic and methodological refinements gradually raised the levels of their generalizations. But few concepts could claim genuine cross-cultural validity and universal applicability. Limited use of data from non-Western societies was made in some of these studies, but the empirical foundations of most of the disciplines remained solidly Western. When the social sciences gained acceptance in non-Western societies, their Western orientation was not significantly altered. Implanted from outside and nurtured somewhat artificially, the social sciences found it difficult to shed their alien character. Even to this day they have not been able to attune themselves to the operating social realities.

The first teachers of many of these disciplines came from abroad, mostly from the home country of the colonial rulers. The textbooks used were also foreign and had little bearing on, or relevance to, the society in which they were used. Most of the earlier researchers were also foreigners who brought with them the conceptual apparatus and methodological tools that had gained academic respectability in their home countries. Native teachers and researchers were trained by these men and often finished their education with a spell of stay and study abroad. Colonial administrators and missionaries—some of them self-taught—also undertook investigations into economic, cultural, and social problems. This as well as much other research was only partly inspired by an academic motivation; it was also an aid to colonial administration.

After the advent of independence in the former colonies and dependencies, it is amazing but true, there was little visible change in the academic culture. The social sciences not only retained their links with high prestige centres of learning abroad, but also maintained, in a significant measure, their attitude of deference, dependency, and servility. Some self-conscious assertions of autonomy notwithstanding, by and large the social scientists of the Third World continued to look up to the great names in Western social science as reference individuals and reference models. Styles set in the academic capitals aboard were avidly copied. There was a race as it were to keep up with the latest trends: imitation of conceptual frameworks and methods of research was all too evident. Little thought was given, in the process, to the applicability and relevance of these frameworks of enquiry and analysis to the countries where they were being adopted most of the developing countries thus remained outposts of academic empires and a sizable group of social scientists continued to function with a captive mind.

In reality, what had happened was the emergence and acceptance of a patron-client relationship between the social scientist of the ore affluent countries and their counterparts in the less developed countries. The system of recognition and reward was weighted in favour of this pattern. Foreign degrees, even from minor universities without any claims to academic excellence, were rated higher than equivalent educational qualifications from the more recognized native centres of learning. Naturally there was a scramble for fellowships and teaching assistantships in foreign universities. Not everyone who entered the portals of these universities came out unscathed; almost all learned something, but some got so enslaved by their new acquisitions that they lost imagination, perspective, and critical ability to identify larger issues of public policy and to explore them unfettered by set ways of thought.

In selections for faculty and research positions, preference was given to those who had published their work in international journals. There was little realization in the less developed countries that the contributions acceptable to these journals possibly required research that did not fit into their own scheme of priorities. Matters of national relevance could leave the editors cold; what they would find exciting might be an academic luxury to a poor country. Books published abroad added tremendously to the reputation of individual scholars; works representing greater depth and persecution published within the country went either run noticed or got acclaim far below the level due to them because of their intrinsic worth. Invitations to international seminars and conferences were another mark of recognition: the more prestigious the centre of learning or sponsoring agency, the greater was the pride of the scholar selected for the distinction. No one wondered *who* got asked and *why*.

Yet another avenue of reward and recognition was participation in international or cross-cultural research projects. The role assigned to the social scientists of the less developed countries in these programmes was often a subordinate one. They did not have a decisive role either in developing the conceptual framework or in determining the methodology of enquiry. They generally collected data to fit into a predetermined framework, following rigidly set methods of investigation. Those who could write and publish in a foreign language occupied the higher echelons of the academic hierarchy; those using native languages were looked down upon. The social science culture, in consequence, retained a satellite character. An astonishingly large number of academics uncritically allowed themselves to be exploited in this subordinate role. Some of them unwittingly even became tools of neo-colonialism and neo-imperialism.

There was a pathetic dependence in the less developed countries on borrowed models and techniques. Great names in contemporary Western social science were shown a degree of reverence that almost bordered on worship. Even the prejudices and predispositions of the mentors abroad were loyally copied. In a sense they, and not the native social scientists, detained what the social sciences should be in the less developed countries. The concepts and theories rooted in and relevant to the Western experience were uncritically applied to the vastly different social situations in the less developed countries. Blind imitations of Western methodology led to distortion of perspectives and falsification of generalizations. For example, in India the individual interview as a tool of research among tribal and rural populations failed to draw reliable responses because people in these societies then to think in groups and prefer to respond with group support, at least when outsiders address to them a series of wide ranging questions. No effort was made to test the reliability and validity of complicated scales and status ladders. In their desire to follow and match the methodological perfection attained elsewhere, these doubtful tools were pressed into service despite their questionable applicability to the situation in the less developed countries. In some instance, studies based on an inadequate conceptual framework and faulty methodology were mechanically repeated several times over. Take, for example, the KAP (knowledge-attitude-practice) studies done in relation to adoption of improved agricultural and new fertility control practices. Several thousand of these studies exist in India alone. The industry displayed was perhaps commendable, but it did not bring forth a single analytic or usable insight.

The consequence of the persistence of these trends was a two-way disaster. The growth of the social sciences remained stunted as the native social scientists operated within parameters set by others and cold not see the challenges and opportunities inherent in their social situation. The results of their imitative research were of doubtful analytic and diagnostic worth because of their inappropriate conceptual and methodological foundations.

The elite of the social scientists in the less developed countries forms a charmed circle, and its members interact mostly with one another and with their peers and mentors overseas. They are very selective even in what they read. Their sources of inspiration and stimulation are confined to a narrowly defined "we group". Contributions of foreign mentors are read and emulated with adulation, and from within the country itself, they read and quote only those who belong to their mutual admiration society.

This pathological and tragic aspect of dependence on outsiders and the failure of their native imitators even to understand their own societies cause no serious concern. They take pride in their "international" status without realizing that they are addressing themselves only to a few hundred people—a select band of professionals. Little effort is made by them to make their voice heard in their own centuries and in the remaining two-thirds of the world consisting of people having comparable low standards of living. The magic of international science, however hollow, continues to cast a strong spell on a sizable section of the Third World social scientists. This so-called international social science needs to be demystified and even debunked because it is based on a false definition of internationalism.

The state of affairs is unsatisfactory and unhealthy. On the national level it leads to setting of wrong priorities and thus to considerable misdirection of effort. As suggested earlier, it also leads to distortions in research findings and their analyses. Because of these inadequacies, the potential of social science in insights and perspectives cannot be fully exploited and pressed into the service of nation-building. In the absence of imagination and creativity, the contributions of the social scientists of less developed countries in the fields of research and reflection neither enrich theory in any significant way nor do they prove powerful aids to social transformation.

The social scientists of the less developed countries mostly write in a foreign language and adopt the esoteric idiom of their discipline. This result in extremely limited diffusion of their ideas in their own countries, and in their inability to contribute significantly to the raising of consciousness among their people.

Another, trend, though it is somewhat unrelated, also deserves to be noted. Although the less developed centuries has a number of problems, the opportunities for them to have a sustained exchange of ideas and experiences are few. Because of the absence of communication and meaningful dialogue among them, a great opportunity of contributing to disciplinary growth both in terms of theory and methods is missed. Paradoxically, we of the Third World see one another mostly through Western eyes. Some of our work indeed finds publication in international journals, but one can legitimately suspect that the chances of its acceptance are enhanced if it follows a pattern. We have remained strangers to each other despite our geographical and cultural proximity and/or the similarity of our tasks and burdens. There is a great deal that can be achieved through indigenization of the social sciences and through evolution of meaningfull patterns of interaction between the social scientists of countries sharing common problems.

The strong urge for the indigenization of the social sciences is not born out of xenophobia, nor is it to be dismissed as a manifestation of national narcissism. Western social scientists have done some good work in the less developed countries and some of them do indeed work jointly with native social scientists on a basis of equality in research endeavors concerning the Third World. Doors do not have to be closed to them and no curtains—of iron, bamboo or paper—have to be raised to bar their participation in research. But some caution is definitely needed. National and foreign spending on social science research must bear a logical proportion; indigenous effort must not be allowed to be swept off its feet by powerful foreign agencies spending lavishly on social research. They should be welcomed as equals, not as masters.

The slavery of mind which blunts the imagination, constricts the vision, and erodes creativity must be fought resolutely. In short, a fresh approach had to be made to invest purpose into the social science endeavour in the less developed countries. The payoff of imitation has been poor. What is needed now is a creative response to our social reality. Rather than be distracted by the glitter of the so-called international social science and blindly follow current fashions, we must take a critical look at the prevailing situation and do something about it.

At the same time, platforms that contribute to productive cross-fertilization of ideas and enhanced interaction amount the social scientists of the less developed countries and other like-minded scholars elsewhere should be created. Indigenization does not involve a retreat of the social science into national shells. It is aimed principally at a redefinition of focus and at purposive efforts to develop dynamic perspectives on national problems and critical issues of public policy.

The emphases in my argument so far have been on the emancipation of the mind and on improving the quality of professional praxis. A number of related arguments in support of the indigenization of the social science can be offered. When they are indigenized, the insider's view of culture and society is likely to emerge in clear relief. This will enable better explication of native categories of thought and of the meaning that the people themselves give. The social sciences, in the process, will relate directly and meaningfully to the country's history, traditions, and corpus of indigenous thought. Such a trend would naturally provide correctives to some of the tragic convolutions of perspective. For example, in a culture-conscious country like India, social anthropologists would not reject tradition and history only because Malinowski and Radcliffe-Brown emphasized the historical character of the discipline, and return to them with zest only when Louis Dumont vigorously pleads for gorging meaningful links between indology on the one hand and sociology and anthropology on the other.

Indigenization would also correct some of the distortions and imbalances in peer group behavior amount the social scientists within the less developed countries. Once the high gods of international social science are dislodge from their pedestals, even those enjoying elite status in their respective countries would take a more serious note of the different approaches and conceptual emphases of those who either do not belong to, or have been kept out of, their closely guarded inner circle.

Finally, subversion by foreign agencies would be held in check, and tragedies like Project Camelot would not be repeated easily. Of course, it would be stupid to treat all foreign researchers as spies, but it would be suicidal to ignore the warnings of possible submersion.

In any debate on the question, all these arguments can be controverter, but their partial validity cannot be demolished. It can be argued that what is assumed or taken for granted by the insider can be brought out in a new and different perspective by the outsider. This is not denied, but even such acceptance does not in any manner diminish the special capability of the insider to illuminate the hidden meanings and subtle nuances of cultural emphases. A return to history and traditions of social and philosophical thought can also vitiate empirical research. That this has happened can be convincingly demonstrated in their new-found love for religious and philosophical traditions as sources for illuminating some of the covert dimensions of culture, many of the recent converts have succeeded only in demonstrating their inadequate familiarity with the classics, and have come out with half-baked and unconvincing propositions.

It is not difficult to anticipate many of the argument against indigenization. The first set of these will revolve around the taxonomic status of the social sciences. Do they have greater affinity with the natural sciences or must we regard them as applied humanities and particle arts? Such an argument need not detain us long. Social sciences do have a special character which is determined by the nature and objectives of their study. Human society cannot be studied like chemical substances, or plants, or frogs and insects.

The second set of arguments will be centered on the propositional structure of science. All sciences, it will be claimed, come out with universalist propositions whose validity can be tested by whites, blacks, yellows, and browns alike, provided they have the requisite training and the minimum infrastructure of investigation. This may be true, but the kind of science practiced in different societies is influenced by a number of dependent variables. Theoretically, the Australian aboriginals are as capable of exploring space and landing man on the moon as the scientists of US and USSR. But will they do it? And must they do it? The practice of science is governed by social needs, and that is why we find differences in how it actually develops in different economic and cultural settings. Besides, not many examples exist of profound universalist propositions of major consequence in the social sciences.

The value neutrality of the social sciences has been done to death. It cannot be denied that objectivity must characterize all science, but the value neutrality of the social sciences will have to be more convincingly demonstrated. Formulations that adopt a self-conscious value-neutral posture can be demonstrated, on deeper analysis, to be founded on value-laden assumptions and are not free from predispositions.

It will be argued that the social sciences are essentially comparative and that their indigenization would detract from this characteristic. This argument has considerable force. However, two points in this context must be borne in mind. First, we must be sure of the quality of what is being compared. Comparisons between distorted and convoluted research findings will be worse than useless. Second, in the first instance at least, like must be compared with like. It is for this reason that a case has been made here for meaningful interaction leading to profitable comparison of the experiences, findings, and trends in the less developed countries. Later the area of comparisons can be exceeded. Much will be lost if we miss the essential first step in this direction.

The very mention of social purpose causes apoplexy among a section of Third World social scientists. With injured innocence, they suggest that all science has its inner logic, and that no one should try to legislate its priorities and directions of growth. Such a view can be ignored, for it is propounded generally by politically naive individuals with little or no social concern. Very little social science can be practiced for its own sake, and no poor country can afford to be indulgent towards the academic luxuries advocated by this self-important group basking in its largely self-evaluated worth. The serendipity pattern underlying all scientific endeavors in to denied. But its acceptance need not necessarily lead to underplaying the obvious. The more pressing problems staring the less developed countries in the face need to be attended to first.

The social sciences in the developing countries stand at a turning point. It is time for serious reflection and redefinition of objectives. The socially-concerned among us have to engage in serious heart-searching. Indigenization of the social science endeavour can provide a way out of the present impasse.

5

COUNTERING AUPANIVESHIK MANSIKTA : SWARAJ AND SWADESHI IN INDIAN SOCIAL SCIENCE*

P.C. Joshi

[For the nationalist thinkers and stalwarts of the cultural renaissance Swaraj was not just freedom from the political domination of the west. it was also "freedom from the colonial domination over the material, mental and moral domain." Nauroji, for example, the first nationalist thinker was also the pioneer of an "autonomous and critical economic approach." It is true that Tagore had rejected nationalism as it had broken up the

---

* The fundamental premises of this paper are that (1) *Swaraj* and Swadeshi were inseparable in the approach of the founding fathers of the Indian renaissance and the leaders of the anti-colonial resistance; (2) and that *Swadeshi* of their conception was opposed not to *Videshi* (i.e., originated in foreign countries) but to *Aupaniveshi* (i.e., having its source in *Aupaniveshik Mansikta* or colonial mentality). Reproduced from *Man* and *Development,* Vol. XIX, No. 1, March 1997.

world into fragments but he also resisted the tendency of the dominant nation to legitimize colonial domination under the false banner of internationalsim or universalism. Similarly, Gandhi was perhaps the first Asian thinker to set a new agenda for Asian social scientists. In 1916 addressing Muir Central College Economic Society Gandhi and upon students and professors to think a fresh on economic issues as Indian conditions were essentially different from that of England. Again, Ranade reminded the Indian social scientists that within the west itself models other than the English economic model existed. An awareness of alternative paradigms could will be the prelude to intellectual Swaraj. The author views the beginnings of "an authentic, Swadeshi Social Science" as part of a larger "fight for Swaraj." —Editor]

India is in danger of losing her soul. She cannot lose it and live. She must not, therefore, lazily and helplessly say, 'I cannot escape the mad onrush of the West'. She must be strong enough to resist it for her own sake and that of the world.

—M K Gandhi, *Young India* 7.10.1926, p. 348

Today it may be said that the original anti-westernism of Gandhi has failed. What is implied that most Indian intellectuals have come to believe that the West is very much with us, that it need not be condemned, that it should be assimilated and that it can be assimilated only if one's cultural roots are strong; that is what Tagore and before him Raja Rammohun Roy and many others of the pre-Gandhi era, had preached and practiced. Nehru's voyage of discovery is very typical of this attitude. Being an attitude, the strands of its beliefs are not so strong as to become convictions and translate themselves into spontaneous action. And being an attitude of such a class, it would spell eclecticism for the majority of the elite. And so it does. To have the best of both the worlds is often indicative of a pre-adult state of mind. The adult stand on their own world to negotiate with the other.

> Judging from conduct apart from verbalization, the Indian intellectual (i.e., social scientist—P C J) does not yet seem fully awakened to his own heritage. He still has to find his moorings.
>
> —D P Mukerji, 'The Intellectual in India', *Diversities*, Peoples Publishing House, New Delhi, 1958, pp. 250-251.

If their quest for relevance to their own societal milieu is to bear fruit under the contemporary pressures for globalization, social scientist must derive sustenance from a fresh search for their indigenous, Indian roots. The deeper the roots in the Indian soil or in the *Swaraj* and *Swadeshi* traditions of the pre-independence era, the stronger the will to soar in the global sky without being blown off by the powerful global winds. In the Asian historical context, the indigenous social science traditions cover a much wider space than that occupied by the contributions of professional social scientists. They encompass the more strategic points occupied by the epoch making, creative thinkers outside the professional domain. To ignore them and their role in the evolution of Indian social science is to deprive social science of much that has helped to pull it out of its colonial conditioning and set it on a creative path in times of great, epochal transitions, as Antonio Gramsci had put it, the influence of a single creative thinker had been far greater and deeper than of all the universities put together (Antonio Grarmsci 1971 : 342). This essay seeks insights into the perspective for social science for the nineties and beyond from a much wider interpretation of social science and its traditions that is conventionally done in professional circles.

I

In order to explore the origins of social science and the basic motivating factors of its growth and development in the non-Western world, one has to explore the deeper nexus between social science and the fight for *Swaraj* defined as the fight against the hegemony of the West. In the Third World countries including India, social science with a distinctly Third World focus and character originated as a societal response to the challenges posed by Western hegemony (colonialism). It was the child of the epoch-making encounter between Western colonialism and resurgent nationalism of the non-Western world. Any alternative explanation of social science growth in terms of exogenous implantation or in terms of the growth of professionalism consequent upon Westernisation of Third World societies is not only partial but also biased and flawed. It contributes little to the illumination on the social conditioning of social science. An integrated view, therefore, must accommodate the creative tensions within the universe of knowledge and the traumatic churning within the societal universe. From this perspective, the contradictory pulls for *indigenization (Swadeshikaran)* under the influence of the fight for *Swaraj* (the search for identity and autonomy) and for *universalization* under the influence of profesionalization within the overall constraints of colonialism, constituted the inner dialectic of social science development in ex-colonial countries including India. To put it differently, genuine indigenization and genuine universalism are not mutually exclusive but mutually re-inforcing processes. But in the context of colonial domination, social science development as an autonomous force was thwarted. Social science in the professional centres could not transcend the distorting influence of the colonial context.

In our view, therefore, any attempt to trace the beginnings of social science growth in terms of transplantation of the Western type of professional centers of social science teaching and research in the Third World produces only a highly biased and untruthful view of social science and its history. It allows social science to be viewed as an extension or an appendage of the social science system of the dominant West and not an autonomous force which challenged the *hegemony* of the West in the realm of generation and dissemination of knowledge and which tried to relate knowledge to the native context. From the point of view of the Western ideologues social science development in the Third World was not an endogenous development. It was promoted by the transfer of social science from the 'intellectually vibrant' West to the 'intellectually moribund' East. From the perspective of the fighters for *Swaraj,* social science development was the result of serious questioning of the assumptions and premises of social science as evolved in the Anglo-Saxon world. It was the result of the quest pioneered by native thinkers for new assumptions and premises corresponding to the native conditions and aspirations and for the indigenization or *Swadeshikaran* of the fundamental scientific approach and concepts developed in the West. *Swarajkaran* for social science has to be understood in terms of rejecting questions posed by Anglo-Saxon ideologues and restating them in the light of the harsh experiences and encounters of the colonized countries and the problems of the non-Western world. In this sense social science was the child of the deep anguish and suffering collectively experienced by the people, which was later transformed into a creative ferment by the intelligentsia of the colonized countries.

Reborn Through an Ordeal

What Jawaharlal Nehru had said about the country being reborn through an ordeal and not through the modernizing influence of foreign rule, applied with equal force to the realm of science and social science. Through such an ordeal a more authentic social science with roots in the indigenous soil was born. As Nehru had put it :

> Out of that tussle and conflict between a nation's soul and a foreign dominating power, modern India took shape. It was a very different India that emerged. The old cringing slavish India was no more and a self-reliant people, conscious of their strength, now faced the world (Jawaharlal Nehru in S. Gopal, 1983: 47).

One can have a full measure of the inner ferment and transformation of social science if one remembers that colonial domination had created conditions for reducing the dependent countries of the East not merely into *economic colonies* of the

West but also into their *intellectual* colonies. Colonial ideology had also exercised a profound influence on social science development, turning social science into an instrument of promoting intellectual subservience. The contrast between dependent Indian and independent Japan also presented a striking contrast between two opposite social situations, one favouring a 'captive' and the other a relatively freer intelligentsia, one favouring a 'thwarted' and the other a relatively autonomous social science growth. The Japanese situation was far more conducive to the indigenization or *Swadeshikaran* of social science than the Indian social situation.

In the above background it is not difficult to understand why the beginnings of the fight against colonialism, that is the fight for *Swaraj,* also constituted the beginnings of an authentic, *Swadeshi,* social science in the Third World. They also mark the beginnings of the struggle between an 'imitative' and an 'innovative' social science approach. The fight for *Swaraj* must be understood in the comprehensive meaning of the term given to it by the founding fathers and the cultural stalwarts of the pre-independence renaissance and nationalist leaders like Dada Bhai Nauroji, M G Ranade and Mahatma Gandhi. We must remember that Dada Bhai Nauroji, who was the first nationalist thinker to have coined and used the term *Swaraj,* was also the pioneer of an autonomous and critical economic approach and the first to link colonialism with India's general socio-economic retrogression and mass poverty. *Swaraj* was thus defined by nationalist thinkers not just as freedom from the political domination of the West. They gave it a broader meaning and deeper content so as to encompass freedom from colonial domination over the material, mental and the moral domain. These leaders were fully aware that it would take a colonized people a much longer time to win their freedom on the material, mental and spiritual plane than it would take them to win it on the political plane. The term *Swaraj,* therefore, subsumed not only economic, social and political liberation; it also encompassed the emancipation of the mind and the spirit. Indeed, the call for independence of mind and spirit was the basic message of the pre-independence renaissance. It implied that *Swaraj* was incomplete without indigenization or *Swadeshikaran* extended to the realm of generation and dissemination of scientific knowledge.

True Modernism is Freedom of Mind

In this thought-provoking lectures on 'Nationalism', even Rabindranath Tagore, who was opposed to narrow nationalism in matters relating to science and culture, had warned against the danger of losing one's autonomy of thinking and judgment which was looming large over the whole of Asia. 'True modernism is freedom of mind, not slavery of taste; it is independence of thought and action, not tutelage under European schoolmasters', observed Tagore (Rabindranath Tagore, 1950:75). These were the words of a sage and a seer who was much ahead of his times and also sensitive, therefore, to the dangers of cultural enslavement. In a fervent appeal to the Japanese people whose creativity was not thwarted by the deadening hand of a colonial state, Tagore had called for a creative and not an imitative response to the questions raised by the West. Tagore had wanted Japan to be the social laboratory for an experiment in evolving and trying out an Asian model of modernity! 'In your voice Asia shall answer the questions that Europe has submitted to the conference of Man', remarked Tagore.

Again, the following wise words addressed to the Japanese nation were in a way addressed to all the Asian nations including the Indian nation :

> The whole world waits to see what this Eastern nation is going to do with the opportunities and responsibilities she has accepted from the hands of the modern time. *If it be a mere reproduction of the West,* then the great expectation she has raised will remain unfulfilled. *For there are grave questions that Western civilization has presented before the world but no completely answered.* The conflict between the individual and the state, labour and capital, man and woman; the conflict between the greed of material gain and the spiritual life of man, the organized selfishness of

> nations and the higher ideals of humanity, the conflict between all the ugly complexities inseparable from giant organization of commerce and state and the natural instinct of man crying for simplicity and beauty and fullness of leisure—all these have yet to be brought to a harmony in a manner not yet dreamt of (Rabindranath Tagore, 1950:57).

Tagore was clear in his mind that the Asian countries 'cannot accept the modern civilization, with all its tendencies, methods and structures and dream that they are inevitable. *You must apply your Eastern mind, your spiritual strength, your love of simplicity, your recognition of social obligations, in order to cut out a new path for this great unworldly car of progress shrieking out its loud discords as it runs.* Reminding the Asian countries about their great and original contributions to the enrichment of human civilization in the past, Tagore had made a very touching appeal not to give in to imitation of the West but to reaffirm Asian individuality :

> Once you did solve the problems of man to your own satisfaction and evolved your own art of living. All this you must apply now to the present situation and out of it will arise a new creation and not a mere *repetition,* a creation which the soul of your people will own for itself and proudly offer to the world as its tribute to the welfare of man (Rabindranath Tagore, 1950 : 57).

We have concentrated on Tagore as the representative figure of Indian Renaissance and not on any other figure because Tagore, unlike Gandhi, was completely free from any anti-West bias. He had rejected even *Swadeshi* as narrow nationalism and had believed in give and take in civilizational matters. Tagore had ruled out any view of East-West as polar opposites, but believed in East-West complementarity and partnership on equal terms. He had upheld 'true modernism' but not aping the European ways in the name of modernizing. Truly like a sage who belonged to no single country but to entire mankind, Tagore had rejected nationalism as a doctrine which must be rejected as 'it had broken up the world into fragments by (erecting) narrow domestic walls'. But he had also rejected the tendency of the dominant national to legitimize colonial domination under the false banner of internationalism or universalism. Even though he was critic of *Swadeshi* in cultural matters, he was a true practitioner of *Swadeshi* in his cultural creations. His entire creative output was inspired by the *Swadeshi* spirit; it was genuinely universal in its appeal because it was truly *Swadeshi* in the sense that it had captured the agony, torments and traumas of the Indian people at a historic moment. It is not without significance that a genuine internationalist like him had felt it necessary to warn against accepting 'the tutelage of the West' and to ask his people to assert their autonomy and independence. It only meant that the compliant and colonial intelligentsia of Asian nations had to be given a moral jolt and that it had to be saved from becoming the docile instrument of imitative Westernization.

By recognizing the threat posed by the Western hegemony, Tagore was not only setting the agenda for activity in the realm of art and culture for the subject peoples of the non-Western world. By re-defining the terms of discourse in terms of the creative expression of Asian autonomy and individuality in the pursuit of 'true modernity' in all fields, Tagore was setting as it were a fresh agenda also for Asian social science. Much before Myrdal and others had talked of the great 'moral discord' within Western civilization, between its ideals and its practice, Tagore had spoken of 'British rule in India as the moral betrayal by the West of its own ideals' (D P Mukerji, 1958: 172) in the naked pursuit of its military, political and economic interests. Much before the Eastern ecologists and humanists had spoken about 'the violence against nature' and 'violence against man' (and woman) as inherent in the Western model of progress, Tagore had made these the central issues of his critique of the West in his lectures on 'Nationalism'. He had asked for an alternative model of progress which would be 'based on *maitri* with nature'. In Tagore's view, the idea of *maitri* was 'at the bottom of Asia's culture' (Rabindranath Tagore, 1950: 73).

Narrow Concept of Progress

In the West, as aptly acknowledged by A N Whitehead, a narrow concept of 'progress' had guided science and social science and had created a situation of confrontation between the world of science and the world of art and culture (A N Whitehead, 1938). Tagore's new vision of 'progress' had created the basis for subsuming science (including social science) within culture on the one hand and culture within science on the other. It is this bridge-building between science, humanities and culture which was an integral part of Tagore's vision for enlightened and emancipated man. It was also a part of the vision of the Indian Renaissance and the struggle for *Swaraj*. This vision was passed on even to the first generation of scientist and social scientist by the pre-independence renaissance and the struggle for *Swaraj*.

Further, Indian Renaissance leaders like Tagore were instrumental in promoting the ethos of self-respect and autonomy in the realm of the mind and the spirit in the same manner as Gandhi was instrumental in promoting it in the realm of politics, ethics and public work, and Jawaharlal Nehru in the realm of nation-building and development. Tagore, Gandhi and Nehru had bequeathed to posterity a new way of measuring true freedom, i.e., *Swaraj*.

As far the ex-colonial countries, it can be said that whether their social science was merely imitative or truly *Swadeshi* (i.e., sensitive to native realities) was an index of the advance made by them in transforming political freedom into *mental Swaraj.* This was so because the damage done by colonialism was more deep-going and enduring in the *mental* sphere than it was in the political sphere. Victims of colonialism had been deprived of the will to think for themselves and to ask to questions relevant for their own situation. True social science must help the 'victim' to become a critic and to enter into a dialogue and discourse on the encounter between the West and the East, not solely on the terms dictated by the West but on terms relevant to the social-existential reality of people in the East. The awakened 'victim' must reset the agenda for enquiry and action in regard to the basic issue of its past, present and future. True freedom would lie in the degree of autonomy exercised in posing and answering the basic question: Was the Western model the only model available to mankind, especially to underdeveloped and dependent countries of the non-Western world, for the pursuit of their material and spiritual well-being?

This was the most vital question that had emerged in the forefront from the encounter between the West and the East, which was not only an encounter between the colonizing West and the colonized East. *Much more significant was the fact that it was also a civilizational encounter between the aggressive and triumphant industrial civilization of the West and the besieged and defensive pre-industrial civilization of the East.* The history of social science development in India and other ex-colonial countries shows that this fundamental question, relating to the social existential reality of the vast millions suffering under colonial oppression, was not raised by the professional social scientists or the Pundits of mainstream Western and Westernized knowledge. We may recall that M K Gandhi, the foremost leader of India's fight for *Swaraj,* had called the universities 'slave-factories', that is producing conformists and not creative human agents.

Tension between the Creative and the Imitative

As a result the heightening of tension between the *creative* and the *imitative,* the *Swadeshi* and the *Aupaniveshik,* orientations in modes of thinking and styles of social praxis was most conspicuous amount the pioneers of the pre-independence renaissance and the philosophers and theoris *of Swaraj,* than among the professional social scientists. The latter were inclined to accept the basic premises of colonial ideology and approach to the problem of the non-Western societies. It is the philosophers and ideologists of *Swaraj* who were from the very beginning engaged in an intellectual confrontation with the ideologies and theories consciously on unconsciously buttressing the notion of the basic inferiority of non-Western civilization *vis-a-vis*

Western civilization. The following words from Gandhi were among the initial first expressions of the autonomy of the mind and spirit in an environment which did not allow any questioning of the hegemony of the West. It is against this slavish intellectual mileu that Gandhi launched his strong protest in the following words :

> My resistance to Western civilization is really a resistance to its indiscriminate and thoughtless imitation based on the assumption that Asiatic are fit only to copy everything that comes from the West (M K Gandhi, 1928: 13).

With Gandhi thus began the tradition of subjecting to critical enquiry Western assumptions and premises, interpretations and judgments, about non-Western societies and civilizations. With Gandhi also began the tradition of questioning and exploding many a myth about the 'modernizing' and 'civilizing' role of colonialism in the non-Western societies, which had been propagated by colonial ideologies. The questioning of certain ingredients of colonialist ideology, that had been initiated by Gandhi's predecessors, was raised by Gandhi to the level of questioning the basic premises of Western civilization itself, which had produced the monster of colonialism. It must also be noted that while sharply questioning the claims of Western ideologies about the superiority of Western civilization, Gandhi had also questioned the Western view of Oriental institutions and values and also the notion that the essential condition of progress was the adoption by the Orient of the institutions and values of the modern West. Gandhi was perhaps the first Asian thinker to set a new agenda for Asian social scientists. In his famous address at a meeting of the Muir Central College Economics Society held on 22 December 1916, Gandhi had 'suggested for the reflection of the economics students and professors that what might be good for England and America need not necessarily be good for India. So he would utter a note of warning that Indian conditions being in some respect so essentially different from the English and the American conditions, it was necessary to bring to bear on the matters that presented themselves to the economists a fresh mind'. What was more important, Gandhi had remarked:

> The economists should first of all examine with patience their indigenous institutions. If they were rotten they must be wiped out and if there were remedies which could be suggested for their betterment, they should improve them (M K Gandhi in Raghavan Iyer 1993: 100).

As we said earlier, Gandhi's most basic and enduring contribution was his critique of Western civilization and of its evils, which overshadowed the good that was also inherent in it. Gandhi's observations on this issue seem to have validity not only for his times but also for our times. The conflict between the evil and the good of Western civilization is as valid today as it was in Gandhi's times. The evil today is represented by the drive in the name of globalization to bring every corner of the earth under the hypnotic spell of the post-modern life-style and its consumerist ethos.

Unfinished Agenda for Mental and Moral Swaraj

In Gandhi's India itself, the national-state, which had been created by the Gandhi-led freedom struggle, has also failed to throw up a model of globalization which would be *Swadeshi* and not *Aupaniveshik* in its motivation and consequences. In this context the following words of Gandhi represent Gandhi's testament, and indeed, an unfinished agenda for *mental and moral Swaraj* as Gandhi had defined. To reproduce Gandhi's highly perceptive and prophetic words:

> I have ventured utterly to condemn modern civilization because I hold that the spirit of it is evil. It is possible to show that some of its incidents are good, but I have examined its tendency in the scale of ethics...Its activity is by no means confined to Europe. Its blasting influence is now being exhibited in full force in Japan. And it now threatens to overwhelm India...1 claim to have tested the life which modern civilization has to give and I cannot help most strongly contesting *the idea that the Indian population requires to be roused by the lash of*

competition and the other material and sensuous, as well as intellectual stimuli. I cannot admit that these will add a single inch to its moral stature (M K Gandhi (1910), in Raghavan Iyer 1993: 89).

It must be frankly recognized that Gandhi's critique of the evils of Western civilization and his call for looking beyond it for India's quest for *Swaraj* had not been accepted in its totality even by such sections of India's intelligentsia as had accepted his political leadership of the anti-colonial struggle and his concept and programme of economic and political *Swaraj*. From the vantage point of today it can be understood that the difference between Gandhi and others was not just of a tactical but of a fundamental nature. Gandhi alone had discerned as a true seer the ominous potential inherent in the evil tendencies of the Western civilization. Others had rejected colonialism but not the Western model of modernity. At best they had spoken of a synthesis between the West and East which, under the conditions of overall Western hegemony, had meant accepting a version of Western modernity modified in the light of Eastern peculiarities. As a result of the basic ambivalence of the Asian elites to the Western model of modernity, Gandhi's influence had at best provided a corrective and an intellectual and moral check against wholesale Westernization. Its full potential for setting ones own agenda in the quest for full and true autonomy had remained largely untapped. One can also pertinently refer to the following penetrating insights of Gandhi having the potential of generating an alternative developement vision and an alternative development paradigm and praxis, which had also remained unremembered and untapped. It is only in the very recent period that these have been rediscovered in the West by ecology and environment philosophers and dissident development thinkers. To quote:

> Nature produces enough for our wants from day to day and if only everybody took enough for himself and nothing more, there would be no pauperism in this world, there would be no man dying of starvation in their world [M K Gandhi (1916), in Raghavan Iyer 1993: 287-288).
>
> The idea of creating an unlimited number of wants and satisfying them seems a delusion and a snare. The satisfaction of man's physical needs, even the intellectual needs of one's narrow self, must meet at a certain point a dead stop, before it degenerates into physical and intellectual voluptuousness (M K Gandhi, 1936: 255-266).
>
> God forbid that India should take to industrialism after the manner of the West. The economic imperialism of a tiny island (England) is today keeping the world in chains. If an entire nation of 300 millions took to similar exploitation, it would strip the world bare like locusts (MK Gandhi, 1928:422).

If through his foregoing observations and other basic insights, scattered in his fittings and speeches, Gandhi had emerged as a deeply perceptive and prophetic economic thinker and pioneer of a new economics and a new economic Utopia, through his basic sociological and political insights on social transformation based on non-violence and the concept of equality and justice, he had also emerged as an original social and political thinker and pioneer of a new sociology and politics and a new social and political Utopia. Indeed, Gandhi had emerged as a powerful bridge between genuine indigenization *(Swadeshikaran)* and genuine universalization of human sciences. There can be no greater confirmation of the true universalism of Gandhi than the fact that the rediscovery of Gandhi and his basic message in our times has begun not in India, the land of his birth and the main social laboratory of his experiments. It has started in the West, which finds in his life and message a new light and hope for mankind in a world engulfed by darkness and despair.

The history of social science evolution in India illustrates both the stimulus for indigenization *(Swadeshikaran)* under the influence of a towering genius like Gandhi and also the thwarting of this indigenization process as a result of the ambivalence to the basic ingredients of Westernism, as displayed by the dominant sections of the Indian educated class.

Despite all these constraints inherent in the Asian situation, one can see, however, the profoundly liberating and stimulating impact of the intellectual challenge to colonialist assumptions and premises offered by the representatives of resurgent Indian nationalism in the pre-Gandhi, Gandhi and the post-Gandhi eras.

We may recall that nationalist thinkers in the pre-Gandhi era had innovated new and relevant concepts and original and novel methods of fact-finding into the actual conditions of 'mass poverty' and general 'retrogression' obtaining in Asian societies under colonial dispensation. Much before the historians and political economists had put the stamp of professional recognition on the concept of 'colonial' economic formation, as a scientific analytical category at par with pre-capitalist (feudal) and capitalist economic formations, the nationalist economic thinkers had already evolved it as an effective tool of political economic enquiry and analysis. As compared to the professional social scientists, who had succeeded the nationalist political and economic thinkers, the latter were far more penetrating, in their grasp of the mechanisms and instrumentalities of politic-economic exploitation and intellectual domination of colonial societies. They had not only offered more meaningful interpretations of social-existential reality of the peoples of colonial societies, within the historical limits set by their times. From the point of view of contributions to the development of social science, their role was indeed path-breaking.

Colonial Ideology and Social Science

Colonial ideology had given a false start to social science by not allowing the right questions to be asked about the causes of India's dependence and thwarted development and also about India's own society, economy, culture and history before the colonial impact. The nationalist thinkers gave the right start to social science by raising for scientific investigation the questions ignored by the colonial ideologues regarding the constraints on Indian growth and development arising from colonialism itself—from the colonial structure, the colonial state and its policies and programmes. So far, the social, economic and cultural history of colonial countries had been written entirely from the standpoint of the colonizing nations; it had rationalized their exploitation and oppression and covered up their real 'interests' and "motivations" by references to their 'civilizing' and 'modernizing' role. From this treatment it would appear that non-Western societies would have remained entrapped forever in backwardness and stagnation if they had not been given the push towards joining the mainstream of civilization by an exogenous force, viz., the revitalizing impact of the West. From the interpretation propagated by colonial ideologues it would appear that far from being 'victims' of colonialism, countries like India were the 'beneficiaries' of the blessings of Western civilization through the mediation of colonial rule.

II

It is not only the blatantly naked ideologues of colonialism who were guilty of a highly biased and flawed view of non-Western societies and their constraints. Some of the most eminent practitioners of professional social science had also acted, however unwittingly, as the promoters of such a biased and flawed view.

What were the basic constraining factors on Indian economic development? This was the question posed about non-Western societies like India, first by colonial ideologues; this was the question which was later asked also by professional social scientists of the West—economists, sociologists and historians. As Sukhamoy Chakravarty points out, in the Indian case because of our connections with Britain starting from East India Company days, through the Imperial days down to the fifties of this century, there was influential group consisting of 'British economists who took an active part in discussions on problems of Indian economic underdevelopment' (Sukhamoy Chakravarty, 1981: 1). The question arises whether the work of these economists, prominent among whom were Alfred Marshall and Vira Anstey provided a corrective or a re-enforcement of the highly biased and flawed colonial slandpoint on India.

Proneness to Oversimplify

It has to be admitted that Vera Anstey was very sensitive to problems of Indian poverty and backwardness and was very sympathetic to the cause of Indian development. As her critique of Mis Mayo's *Mother India* had showed, she did not 'indict the whole Indian nation' but only 'the institutions and customs of certain communities for their role in thwanting the development process in India. And yets 'inspite of all her sympathy for India', remarked Sukhamoy Chakravarty. Anstey nowhere saw any merit in the nationalist case, which after all was a critique of British Imperial rule. Here failure as well as the failure of British thinking during this period was finally reducible to 'a total rejection of a model of complex and contradictory process of change which the British imprint had generated in India. It is here that a proper conceptualization of the dynamics of an evolving world economy since the late seventeenth century was most needed, a point not grasped by Vera Anstey in repeatedly comparing India with medieval Europe' (S Chakravarty 1989: 7). Vera Anstey's view regarding prerequisites of industrial and agricultural development showed a proneness to oversimplify a complex process. In her book, *Indian Economic Development,* Vera Anstey observed as follows in regard to conditions of industrial progress:

> "It has been said that four things are required to be found to establish an industry successfully in

> any country—men, money, materials, and markets. If to these is added motive power, the saying may be considered to sum up the prerequisites of industrial production" (Vera Anstey, 4th Edition 1952: 277).

In regard to agriculture Vera Anstey was of the view that 'the methods of organization and remuneration of labour which give no spur to increased effort are chiefly responsible for the low output per head but one aggravated by the enervating climate and the prevalence of debilitating diseases' (Vera Anstey, 1952: 15).

It is obvious that Vera Anstey's attention is concentrated on what W A Lewis called 'the proximate causes of growth', while completely ignoring 'the causes of these causes' including the total institutional framework of industry and agriculture.

Alfred Marshall, despite his much greater eminence and stature as a theoretician and economic analyst, had also failed to provide adequate clues for identifying the constraints on Indian economic development. In a letter to his former student, Manoharlal, written in 1909, he had presented an oversimplified view of these constraints. Marshall had remarked:

> I do not believe that any device will make India a prosperous nation, until educated Indians are willing to take part in handling *things* as

> educated people in the West do. The notion that it is more dignified to hold, a *pen* and keep accounts than to work in a high grade engineering shop seems to me the root of India's difficulties (A C Pigou, 1956:456-457).

In the above extract, Marshal had no doubt presented a penetrating insight into the dominant social attitude acting as a constraint on development. From hindsight the value of his insight appeared far greater than it would have appeared to the nationalists engaged in a polemic with the colonial ideologues. And yet Marshal was inclined to overlook that this social attitude was not just a constraint inherited from the pre-colonial past. It was constraint extended from the top layer of Indian society to the society at large by the colonial system of education and colonial policies of deindustrialisation. If this attitude still persisted, it was because in large parts of India the colonial system of education was still dominant; and government service still constituted the preferred employment by the educated class. No serious attempt had been made to break this vicious circle. Colonialism had no doubt gone but the habits formed during a century and half of colonial rule had not disappeared with colonial rule.

Again, in a letter to another student, B Mukerjee of Lucknow University, Marshall had remarked:

> For twenty years I have been urging Indians in Cambridge to say to others: How few of us when

we go the West think of any other aim save that of our individual culture? Does not the Japanese nearly always ask himself in what way he can strengthen himself *to do good* service to his country on his return? Does he not seek real studies? *Does he not watch the sources of Western Power?* Is not that the chief reason of Japan's quick progress? Cannot we imitate her? (A C Pigou, 1956: 472).

In the above letter to his student, Marshall appeared as a true scholar free from the least trace of colonial pride and prejudice. He appeared deeply sympathetic to the cause of Indian development and also earnest about promoting the human agents for it *via* training of Indian economists. And yet his statement betrayed a singular lack of insight into the constraints imposed by colonialism in India. His Indian students were not as free to practice what Marshall preached in the India of that period as Japanese students were in Japan of the Meiji Restoration and thereafter. While Indian educated in England turned into political agitators after their return to their country, the Japanese students turned into active agents of development. Marshall had overlooked against that colonialism was also at the root of many difficulties faced by Indian students to make practical use of their training as economists. Why is it that even today students studying in England and America did not show the same eagerness to take their newly acquired skills available to their own country for its economic progress as the Japanese and Chinese students did was a question which must be posed. This raises the question of the character of the Indian middle class and the conditions which have moulded this character.

In the context of our discourse on social science and on the constraining as well as liberating influences on Indian social science, the following cryptic summing up by Chakravarty was very apt as well as relevant:

> Perceptions of British economists sympathetic to India demonstrate that as long as the Imperial rule lasted, *there were major limitations imposed on the cognitive process by social conditioning based on an unequal relationship* (Sukhamoy Chakravarty, 1989: 7).

Had 'the major limitations imposed on the cognitive process by social conditioning based on an unequal relationship' vanished after the end of direct colonialism? Or, to the extent that 'unequal relationship' between the West and a large part of East was still a fact of life, the 'limitations imposed on the cognitive process' by this relationship were still in force, even though they might have assumed different forms and shapes? These issues deserved fresh examination in the context of today when 'relationship' between the West and a large part of the East especially in the intellectual sphere, had become far more unequal for the Third World countries than ever before. It must be noted that our understanding of the development possibilities and constraints in India was still subject to 'social conditioning based on an unequal relationship'. Not only the perceptions and prescription by certain sections of the intellectual elite but the preferred options and policy packages which were presented as fruits of original thinking today could be discerned as 'old wine in new bottles'—the Alfred Marshall-Vera Anstey perceptions and prescriptions of yesterday as new insights and panaceas of today.

Deep Pessimism about Underdeveloped

'Why are we rich and they so poor? This was the question posed by 19th century Western economic analysts and commentators. This was the question which was still being asked by Western economists during the nineties of the present century' (David S Landers 1990: 1-12). And the outlook of underdeveloped countries as perceived by some of the Western economists was as grim as it appeared to the 19th century commentators. In the Richard T Ely Lecture by David S Landers we confront as it were Alfred Marshall and Vera Anstey in a new garb—more sophisticated and more glamorous - but perhaps without the warm sympathy on the latter for the economically weak and the dependent. The deep pessimism about the prospects for underdeveloped countries was, however, the common assumption despite the time interval of more than half a century.

Encountering the influence still exercised by 'the unequal relationship' on the 'cognitive process' was perhaps the greatest challenge facing social scientists of the erstwhile Third World today. There is not doubt that the complex environment for Third World development in the contemporary setting requires a far more sophisticated conceptualization of the dynamics of an evolving world economy and of India as part of this world than what was provided by the approach and conceptual framework of nineteenth century and early twentieth century nationalist thinkers. But if the nineteenth century nationalist thinking was obsolete in certain respects the Marshall-Vera Anstey perceptions and prescriptions and their present versions are equally obsolete from the point of view of identifying the real constraints and possibilities of the Third World countries. And Yet, as B N Ganguli had argued, in understanding the basic nature of the Indian problem, the insights provided by nationalist thinks have more enduring illuminating power than the Alfred Marshall-Vera Anstey type of interpretations of social reality of underdeveloped countries or their contemporary versions.

III

It remains to be seen in what respects the perceptions of the nationalist economic thinkers were different from those of the Western economists who had represented the enlightened view of the Western social science of that period. It also remained to be seen how far the nationalist viewpoint was valid today and, if not, what major revisions did it require in the vastly altered world of today.

As noted earlier, during the nineteenth and early twentieth century Calcutta had emerged as the cultural metropolis of India, leading creative reawakening in art and culture. During the same period Bombay in Western India had emerged as the leading centre of creative thinking and praxis in the fields of politics and economics. If the Bengal Renaissance contributed in a large measure to the *indigenization* (Swadeshikaran) *of the cultural perspective,* the West Indian renaissance had contributed to the *indigenization* (Swadeshikaran) *of political thought and praxis on the one hand and* economic thought and praxis on the other. Both the Bengal Renaissance and the West-Indian Renaissance had contributed enomously in lurning the winds of the intelligentsia of the colonial period towards the guest for true modernism.

Process of 'Creative Destruction'

Ranade thus gave a new meaning to *Swadeshi* thinking—*Swadeshi* in the sense not of inventing new and original principles and concepts of science but *Swadeshi* in the sense of selective and critical borrowing from the vast stock and flow of knowledge available in dynamic parts of the Western world and applying it to Indian conditions through appropriate modifications, adaptation and reconstruction. Ranade, in fact, had illustrated how the process of 'creative destruction' yielded better insights than that of mechanical application of Anglo-Saxon concepts to Oriental conditions. His own essay on 'Indian Political Economy' and his other writings exemplified this method of *Swadeshi* thinking.

Gandhi, who had given legitimacy to the concept of *Swadeshi* and who had the appearance of an anti-Western thinker to a much greater extent than any other Indian thinker of the modern world, was also *Swadeshi* in this fundamental sense and not in the sense and the meaning that is attributed to him by those exploiting the concept of *Swadeshi* for political purposes to-day. Gandhi had drawn very much upon the dissident Western thinkers like Rousseau, Thoreau, Emerson, Risking and many others had assimilated their insights and for the reconstruction of his own intellectual worldview and his own methodology.

It must be appreciated that Indian nationalist economic thinkers had original contributions to development thinking and for want of a better term they can all be put in the category of *Indian Institutionalists.* While *institutionalism* had emerged as a dissident trend in the Western tradition, as a protest against mainstream development thinking, Asian Institutionalism in the era of the fight for

Swaraj had emerged as the mainstream of Swadeshi development thinking relevant for the underdeveloped, ex-colonial counters. It was not Gunnar Myrdal *of Adsian Drama* but M G Ranade, M K Gandhi and Others who had pioneered the *Institutional Approach* to Development in Third World countries like India. The Ranade, Gokhale and Gandhi tradition was carried forward by social science stalwarts like Radhakamal Mukerjee, D.R. Gadgil, Anjaria and Nanavati, Brij Narayan and Gyan Chand, who had founded and built *Swadeshi* social science Schools within Indian Universities. One of the major failures of the Social Scientists of the post-colonial India is illustrated by their general indifference to this and their failure to vigorously carry forward the tradition of *Swadeshi* thinking at the level of approach, concept and methods and to build an elegant theoretical edifice on the foundations provided by the Indian Institutionalists of the era of the fight for *Swaraj* and *Swadeshi*.

The major intellectual challenge for the Indian Institutionalists was to explain the phenomena of social-economic stagnation and mass poverty under colonial rule. It was to explain why, despite its vast growth potential, India was one of the most backward and poverty-stricken regions of the world. Was the key to this riddle provided by Indian's growth-retarding institutions and values inherited from the pre-colonial period as the colonial theorist claimed? Or was the explanation to be found in the role of the colonial state which had imposed retrograde institutions and values on the native environment and adopted economic policies with the main objective of promoting the interests of the mother country at the expense of autonomous development of the colony? Any disinterested and non-partisan analyst of the Indian economic problem would agree that in this confrontation between colonial theorists and commentators on the one hand and nationalist economic thinkers on the other, the latter had provided much deeper insights in the processes of 'cumulative causation' resulting in India's mass poverty and backwardness. Indeed, as we show later, Ranade's essay on *Indian Political Economy* was qualitatively superior both as a theoretical and an applied exercise to the observations on the Indian economic problem offered by Alfred Marshall or to the more intensive treatment by Vera Anstey.

Interdependence of Development of Industry and Agriculture

One can recall Ranade's theoretical refutation of the prescription of orthodox English economists 'assigning to the backward tarried zone regions of Asia the duty of producing raw materials and to the advanced European zone countries the work of transport and manufacturers as a territorial division of labour which is fraught with the highest advantage to all' (M G Ranade, 1916: 23-24). One can recall also his brilliant insight into the interdependence of development of industry and agriculture. Ranade had argued how, consequent on deindustrialization, 'ruralization' in modern India, a distinctly retrograde move, had taken place very fast, resulting in India's 'justification, i.e., a loss of power and intelligence, and self-independence' (M G Ranade, 1916: 26-27). Ranade had also contrasted the total indifference of the colonial state to its development-promoting function and responsibility which, according to him, had become the central premise of modern economic thought even in European countries like France and Germany. In his view, '*the state is now more and more recognized as the national organ for taking care of all national needs in all matters in which individual and co-operative efforts are not likely to be so effective and economical as national effort. The pioneering of new enterprises is a duty which the government might more systematically undertake with advantage.* There is, lastly, the duty cast on it of utilizing indigenous resources and organizing them in a way to produce in India in state factories all products of skill which the state departments require in the way of stores' (M G Ranade, 1916: 33). Ranade had thought that this was the only logical course to be adopted 'only if the minds of rulers were once thoroughly freed from the fear of offending the so-called maxims of rigged economical science' (M G Ranade, 1916: 33).

Ranade had attached much greater importance to the development-promoting function of the state in India than in European countries because of the fact that in India 'there is almost complete absence of a landed gentry or wealthy middle class' (M G Ranade, 1916: 22). Ranade had further clarified that the function of the state was 'to help these influences which tended to secure national progress through the several stages of growth, *and adopt free trade or protection* as circumstances may require. In this view free trade may be good for a country like England, but not for America and Germany' (M S Ranade, 1916: 19).

Ranade's Concept of State-led Industrialization

If one was not told that the above observations were authored by Ranade, one would in the natural course associate these views and the grand conception of state-led economic development with Jawaharlal Nehru. For the purpose of *historical* record it must be clearly understood that the father of economic nationalism and the nation-state-led industrialization was not Jawaharlal Nehru but Mahadev Govind Ranade. *Nehru, the head of the newly formed Indian nation-state, had only put into operation in 1958 the prescription which had been formulated and presented by M G Ranade in his lecture delivered at the Deccan College in 1892.*

Ranade had showed a remarkable insight into the exogenous constraints on Indian economic growth imposed by British colonialism. He had also showed a keen perception of the institutional constrains inherited from the pre-colonial period. To quote:

> The characteristics of our social life are the prevalence of status over contract, of combination over competition. Our habits of mind are conservative to a fault. Our laws and institutions favour a low standard of life and encourage subdivision and not concentration of wealth. The religious ideas of life condemn the ardent pursuit of wealth as a mistake to be avoided as far as possible. These are *old legacies* and *inherited weaknesses*. Stagnation and dependence, depression and poverty—these are written in broad characters on the face of the land and its people. To these must be added the economical drain of wealth which foreign subjection has entailed in the country (M G Ranade, 1916: 23).

Ranade, however, did not consider the transfer of English institutions and motivations centered on rejection of altruism and on pursuit of naked self-interest as essential conditions for economic growth in India. In his view, application of the comparative method yielded prescriptions of a different kind. Ranade had clearly stated that 'the basis of a *hypothetical economic man guided solely by one motive of self-interest must be given up on man, as he is both selfish and altruistic, possessing rights as well being bound by duties,* must be studied in history, both ancient and modern'. Again Ranade asserted that 'universalism and perpetualism in economic doctrine are both unscientific and untrue' (M G Rande, 1916: 20).

In the following passage Ranade was more eloquent and emphatic in his plea for breaking away from the dogmas of orthodox economics. Ranade had observed:

> Modern European thought does not countenance the view of the English writers that the principles of the science, as they have enunciated them in their text books, are universally and necessarily true for all times and places and for all stages of advancement. *Modern thought is veering to the conclusion that the individual and his interests are not the centre round which the theory must revolve, that the true centre is the body politic of which the individual is a member, and that collective defense and well being, social education and discipline and the duties and not merely the interests of men, must be taken into account, if the theory is not to be merely Utopia.* The method to be followed is not the deductive but the historical method, which takes account of the past in its forecast of the future; and relativity not absoluteness, characterized the conclusion of economic science (M G Ranade 1916: 21).

In a brilliant, cryptic summing up of his view Ranade had remarked: 'The laws of social progress in wealth must be sought in the history of the general social evolution which is different in different countries' (M G Ranade 1916: 11).

Ranade's Development Thinking Far Ahead of Contemporaries

It was not Adam Smith's economic thinking centered on primacy to the 'individual' and his pursuit of his 'naked self-interest' and on unfettered freedom to him from state intervention an interference that corresponded to the requirements of a country like India which was a late-comer to development and also lacking in political sovereignty and the opportunity to chart out a course suited to its own interests. It was the writings of Frederic List of the German Historical School, 'which gave the fullest expression to the rebellion against orthodox English (Smithian) creed', on whom Ranade relied for theoretical support for his thinking on constraints and possibilities of Indian economic development. It was List who had intellectually spearheaded the transition from the era of 'individual' as the unit to that of *'nation' as the unit* and from the individual as the entrepreneur to the nation-state as the pioneer leading the entrepreneurial revolution. As Sukhamoy Chakravarty had reminded us, 'classical economics had no conceptual category called 'a nation' and that innovation belonged to List' (Sukhamoy Chakravarty, 1988; III). We must also remember that in England, which was the pioneer of the modern Industrial Revolution and the typical economic laboratory for the doctrine of lassez faire, national sentiment, nationalism and the national-state, had followed rather than preceded the Industrial Revolution. It was not in England but in the late-comer continental countries, where the concept of 'nation as the unit' and nation-state as the propeller of the development process originated. It was Ranade's historical contribution to build his theoretical argument on the postulates provided not by Adam Smith and his successors but by Frederick List. Ranade's development thinking was, therefore, much ahead of that of the English or Indian economists of the colonial era, who were guided by the Smithian doctrine in their understanding of India's economic problem.

There are many both on the Right and the Left who think that the concept of planning, with the states as its main instrument, originated with Marx and later found in Lenin its great patron and promoter. This conventional view has now been contested by many scholars. The British historian, E H Carr, for instance, had argued that Lenin had borrowed the concept of planning from Frederick List who was its originator. Nearer home, many in India had also believed that it was predominantly under the influence of his exposure to Fabian socialism and to the example of the Soviet Five year plans Nehru, the Chairman of the National Planning Committee had become the protagonist of the interventionist state and 'planned economy'. One of the most eminent development economists, Jagdish Bhagwati had also traced of the influence of 'Fabian-type socialism' and of 'soviet example' to Nehru and via Nehru on India's intellectuals and it sobering elite (Jagdish Bhagwati, 1985: 89-60). The fact of the matter is that Ranade, the economic thinker and publicist, had already created, through his writings and speeches, the intellectual climate of opinion favouring the leading role of the state in development. This concept of state leadership approximated to what later was called state-directed economic planning. Thus, Nehru, the executive head of the post-colonial state, was the continuator of Ranade's grand conception of the nation-state as the motive force for India's social and economic regeneration rather than its principal originator and architect. This notion of a nation-state had emerged from historical compulsions of an anti-colonial revolution, which had as its objective the replacement of the colonial state by the nation-state. The national revolution had envisaged the nation-state to be the main instrument of putting into effect the programmed of transforming a dependent economy into an independent, self-reliant economy.

Concept of State-led Development Well Thought Out

Thus, this notion of state-led development itself was not an idea mindlessly transplanted on the Indian soil. It had been critically reviewed, well-thought out, and assimilated by the intellectual elite.

It had also been legitimized through a long process of national dialogue and discourse. Whether Nehru was aware of it or not, he was standing on the shoulders of his predecessor, M G Ranade, who himself had derived this notion from List and then adapted it to Indian conditions.

Nehru had further modified on critical points Ranade's statistic conception which had been evolved within the limits imposed by his times. Nehru tried to recast this grand view in the light of mid-twentieth century compulsions of consolidating the post-colonial nation-state on the one hand and meeting the challenges created by the democratic political system and the Constitution in term of the uplift and well-being of the vast masses on the other.

What we are trying to emphasize is that M G Ranade and others, who went beyond the classical liberal orthodoxy and its neo-classical versions, had offered far more illuminating and penetrating perceptions of India's constraints and possibilities than social scientists who had remained imprisoned in liberal orthodoxy and its neoclassical variants.

The Ranade-Nehru vision and their line of thought and action, centered on the leading role of the nation-state in development, had the most profound influence on social science outlook and agenda during the mature phase of the anti-colonial struggle and in the post-colonial era. It is this vision and its line of thought and action which is now under attack from inside and outside. Where do we go from here? What new indigenous vision, new lines of thought and action are taking its place? Or, are we in the process of being overwhelmed 'by alien ideas which may have little or no relevance to the socio-economic situation in the country' (B N Ganguli, 1977: x). As we said earlier, in the preferred options and policy-packages emanating from the West and its leading institution overseeing development performance of the Third World, we find not original thinking but perhaps an echo of the Alfred Marshall-Vera Anstey perceptions and prescriptions of yester-years. Is it a forward movement or a regression in fundament terms? This is an issue which is not easy to resolve.

IV

To sum up, we cannot cope with the issues and challenges confronting India during the nineties and beyond and resolve where we have to make a drastic break from the past without first resolving the tension between continuity and change. This is a task which must be taken up by economist, social historians, sociologists and political scientists of the new era. To what extent the interpretations of the concepts of Swadeshi Swaraj of the anti-colonial and the post-colonial era all suited to the new social situations of India during the nineties? To what extent did the interpretations of these concepts, which originated in the context of external colonialism and were a response to the challenges posed by colonial ideology in the sphere of social science, also encompass the challenges posed by 'inner colonialism' and by the inner cleavages and contradictions within the Indian society itself? To what extent did Swaraj encompass the interests and aspirations of the subaltern classes, communities and regions and to what extent did Swadesh and Swadeshi challenge the hegemony of the haves over the have-nots, the classes over the masses, males over females, and the literati over those excluded from literacy in the comprehensive sense of the term? In other words, what are the constraints of intellectual legacy discussed above, of the outlook and concepts associated with Swaraj and Swadeshi, which have their roots in the historical milieu in which they originated? These questions which are crucial for our quest for a new perspective on social science for the nineties will be addressed in a separate paper.

We have raised these questions at the end only to indicate that while recognizing the historical role of the interpretations of the concepts of *Swaraj* and *Swadeshi,* which were thrown up by the Indian Renaissance and the anti-colonial resistance, we are also aware of their serious limitations and deficiencies from the point of view of our emerging challenges and contradictions today. At the same time the Gandhi-Tagore dialogue, the Gandhi-Nehru debate, the highly perceptive Gandhi-Ambedkar debate, the Gandhi-Nehru left dialogue, the Nehru-

Jayaprakash-Lohia dialogue to name only a few, were also indicative of the wider and not the narrow meaning of concepts of *Swaraj* and *Swadeshi* which began to dominate the thought and praxis of the latter-day managers of the nation-state. Moreover, the creative ferment in Indian society was not restricted to the movements led by the *Swadeshi* and *Swadeshi* leaders. It also encompassed social reform movements and cultural currents in different regions pioneered by activists and reformers from subaltern classes, about whose role official history is completely silent and indifferent. It is these movements and currents which had broadened the meaning of *Swaraj* and *Swadeshi.* It must not be overlooked that the degeneration of the concept of *Swaraj* as legitimization of the self-aggrandizement of a minority and the appropriation of *Swadesh* by a self-seeking and self-serving centralized elite, resulting in the alienation of the working people from *Swaraj* and *Swadesh,* was not inherent in the original concepts of *Swaraj* and *Swadeshi.* It is these original, wider interpretations of the concepts of Swaraj and Swadeshi which need to be taped now to build bridges between *Swadeshi* and *Swaraj* valid for yesterday and *Swadeshi* and *Swaraj* relevant for today and tomorrow. These wider connotations and meanings of these historically evolved terms are capable of reorienting themselves in response to the dynamic processes of history-in-the making. Such creative redefinition alone can resolve the current tension between regression and forward movement.

References

1. Jagdish Bhagwati, *Wealth and Poverty,* Essays in Development Economics, Vol. I, Basil Blackwell, Oxford, 1985.
2. Chakravarty, Sukhamoy, 'British Perceptions of Indian Economic Problems: Dr. Vera Anstey and Her book', *The Indian Economic Journal,* Vol. 37, No. 2, October-December 1989, pp. 1-7.
3. Chakravarty, Sukhamoy, 'Reflections on the Economic Perspectives', in *In Search of India's Renaissance,* Vol. 2, Centre for Research in Rural and Industrial Development, Chandigarh, 1992, pp. 109-112.
4. Ganguli, B N, *Indian Economic Thought Nineteenth Century Perspectives,* Tata-McGraw Hill Co. Ltd., New Delhi, 1977.
5. Gandhi, M K, *Young India,* January 12, 1928.
6. Gandhi, M K, in *Harijan,* August 29, 1928.
7. Gandhi, M K, in *Young India,* December 20, 1928.
8. Gadgil, D R 'Gokhale as an Economist', *Writings and Speeches,* Orient Longman Ltd., New Delhi, 1981, pp. 243-259.
9. Iyer, Raghavan (ed.), *The Essential Writings of Mahatma Gandhi,* Oxford University Press, New Delhi, 1993.
10. Joshi, P C, *Social Science and Development: Quest for Relevance,* Har-Anand Publication, New Delhi, 1995.
11. Landers, David S, 'Why are We Rich and they so Poor', Richard T Ely Lecture, *American Economic Review,* Vol. 80, No. 2, 1990, 1-12.
12. Pigou, A C (ed.), *Memorials of Alfred Marshall,* Kelley Reprints, New York, 1956.
13. Tagore, Rabindranath, *Nationalism,* Macmillan and Co. Limited, London, 1950.
14. Whitehead, A N, *Science and the Modern World,* Penguin Books Ltd., 1938.

6

SCIENCE AND SWARAJ*

J.P.S. Uberoi

[Uberoi believes that the advancement of science in India cannot be separated from advancement of independence, for "the problems of science in a rich, technologically satiated society are different from its problems in a poor soeity of lately liberated from colonial bondage." And the so called scientific internationalism is meant to uphold western dominance in all matters of scientific life and organization. Uberoi backs his formulation by referring to the problem of sociological/ anthropological studies in India. While N.K. Bose believed that the malady of anthroplogical studies is largely colonial, i.e., European or American, Indian scholars simply see it as an intellectual failure – an inability to make an original contribution. It must be said to Uberoi's credit that he starkly sees and boldly states the causal connection between

*From *Contributions to Indian Sociology* (h.s., 1968, 2)

the colonial bondage and the lack of originality. —Editor]

The aim and method of science are no doubt uniform throughout the world but the problem of science in relation to society is not. The problem or problems of science in a rich, technologically satiated society are different from, even opposed to, its problems in a society of poverty lately liberated from colonial bondage. The two sets of problems and two situations cannot, without serious falsification, be placed upon a single continuum. It is scientism and not science which conceives of them along the single line of unlinear evolutionism. Our understanding of the proper content of science, its problems and its priorities in relation to a specific society will depend on our attitude toward this question.

Certain evident discontinuities, oppositions and relations in the real world must be considered if we are ever to conceive of our science from our point of view correctly. The sociology of knowledge is a study of urgent practical importance today, for some consideration of it should form the prolegomenon and background to the determination of particular priorities and objectives.

I believe that the advancement of science in India cannot be separated from the advancement of independence. The end of our intellectual and practical apprenticeship in science is long overdue by any sensible reckoning, but we are constantly cajoled or browbeaten to prolong it for one reason or other.

We can be frustrated by force where we cannot be contained by stratagem and system. Such things are done to poor nations and peoples today, in science as in politics, in the new fashion of a false cosmopolitanism and false humanitarianism, not in the old terms of colonial tutelage or racism. The latter ideologies emphasized discontinuities and hateful ones, while nowadays all talk is of brotherhood, harmony and sweet reasonableness, but the effects are not totally dissimilar. The nuclear non-proliferation treaty, in effect poised to subvert both our science and our independence, is a characteristic product of the new era, combining humbug and coercion in equal proportions.

As a social institution science, national or international, cannot and does not live outside its area. It is no different in this regard from other human institutions. The twin facts of the terrible potency of the rich and the helpless squalor of the poor among nations constitute the unitary framework, the primary opposition of our technocratic age. The chasm is fixed between us and them. There is no "world community of science", unless that phrase be another name for the national and international science of rich nations. Scientific internationalism is a bridge of illusion, a cloak of comfort across the chasm. The existing system of foreign aid in science, to which the internationalist notion of collaboration lends credence, in truth upholds the system of foreign dominance in all matters of Scientific and professional life and organization. It is nothing but the satellite system, with an added subsidy. It subordinates the national science of the poor to the national and international science of the rich. It confirms our dependence and helplessness and will not end them. The reasons for these effects is simple and fundamental : the national and the international systems inherently are synonymous for the rich but opposites for the poor. This relativism is the iron law of international collaboration.

I certainly am aware that it is tabooed to bring up such matters at scientific conferences, even when they are ostensibly called to consider them, or discuss them in scientific journals. A deep silence is liable to descend on all sides if someone broaches the unpalatable truth. Permit me to quote in this connection the illustrious name of Claude Levi-Strauss and the events of a planning conference on urgent anthropology that was held in Washington in 1966. During his lucid address of September 17, 1965 to the Smithsonian Institution, which apparently had inspired the idea of the conference and copies of which were provided to all participants (Sturtevant 1967 : 355c-356a), the great Frenchman had spoken of the ambience of anthropology and sought to draw certain implications for its future. He had said that anthropology is the outcome of a historical process which had made the larger part of mankind subservient to the smaller and thrown millions into bondage. "Anthropology is daughter to this era of violence" (Levi-Strauss 1966 : 126a). He therefore doubted if there can exist any real "reciprocity of perspective" between the two unequal halves of mankind, lately in the relation of exploiters and exploited, for : "Between our attitude toward them and their attitude toward us, there is and can be no parity" (ibid. : 125b-126a). He went on to explain the likely consequences for anthropology in our time.

Now, what happened when the international conference of 48 anthropologists from 22 countries met, with these considerations before it ? The deliberations of the conference calmly ignored the distinction which Levi-Strauss had sought to make, be it noted, by simply "failing to consider his reasons", as the official record puts it (Sturtevant 1967: 356b). Instead of facing the unpleasant truth, or considering the sociology of science, "attention was devoted (although not explicitly in these terms) to means for making anthropology more palatable" *(ibid:* 356b).

It is the way of internationalism and international science always to draw the sting of conflict by acknowledging the role of oppositions and contrarieties in pure thought nature, while reducing the real conflicts and struggles of making to meaningless formulae. I refer to the report of Ralph

L. Beals of international research problems and ethics as an example of the prevalent style. It is the familiar jargon of "international anthropology", complete with "international exchanges", "cooperation" and "two-way cross-cultural research" (Beals 1967 : 473a-474a). Almost in passing Beals writes of the former human subjects of anthropology that they were studied partly because "they were clearly apt to disappear shortly" *(ibid:* 470b). This formula is the new bland euphemism of international social science for genocide committed and connived at by rich and powerful governments. I fully expect to be told soon in the same vein that, when the Jews were clearly apt to disappear, afew far-sighted Nazi scientists took the final opportunity to enhance human knowledge by making an experiemental study of them. Such sophistry is the inevitable result of discussing international problems and ethic without reference to the structure of concrete reality.

Let us return to India. A little research will show that there are two ways of formulating the present position of anthropological or sociological studies in India. (1) Nirmal Kumar Bose says, "The position of Indian anthropology has, on the whole, been colonial in relation to Schools which have dominated the European or American scene from time to time" (Bose 1963: 46 *quoted in* Ferreira 1967 : 77). Unfortunately I find that this is the minority view. Most people, on the contrary, prefer to say : (2) Indian scholars, on the whole, have not as yet made an original and significant contribution to the development and refinement of international anthropology (or sociology or whichever other science). The two modes of expression lead to two quite different trains of thought and action.The Bose formulation, as I see it, puts the emphasis on decolonialization. It leads us to wonder why the "colonial relation", broken in politics, persists in science. The second formulation by subtly shifting the emphasis to "originality", which is a pseudo-problem, obfuscates the issue and paralyses action. At best it will make us run with borrowed money to attend the next international conference to learn how to be original.

We are so accustomed to the second mode of thought that John V. Ferreira, who quotes the Bose formulation, in fact understands it as a candid confession of "sterility" (Ferreira 1967: 77). A simple transformation perhaps but one in which the "colonial relation" has disappeared from view altogether. Virility, supposing that we had ever possessed any, is lost without focus and object.

In deference to high fashion, I should perhaps express the matter as a formula, apparently passionless. In my view then:

LEVI-STRAUSS : BEALS : : BOSE : FERREIRA

This appears to be succinct enough but it is at the same time too concrete a summary. Another reference to Beals's view will explain the issues better. I find that in terms of his categorization I am one of the misguided few who, in plain words, "place national interests, as they conceive of them, above the international values of anthropology" (Beals 1967: 472b). (Apparently Beals expects the black sheep to be found in closed rather than open societies but that only proves how thoroughly all sheep, black and white, are brainwashed washed nowadays.) And what are the international values of anthropology? It appears that there are two : "contributing to the improvement of the art of government and the betterment of the human condition" *(ibid:* 472b). Here we have the matter in a nutshell. If you pursue these noble and laudable aims within the internationalist framework, then you are pure and white, like the nuclear non-proliferationists. If you pursue the same aims but within the nationalist framework, then you are dissident and black.

I therefore conclude the argument with the following set of oppositions which are structurally equivalent:

RICH : POOR : : INTERNATIONAL :
NATIONAL : :
WHITE : BLACK

This is the matrix of science and swaraj in today's world seen from our point of view. Every swarajist should recognize what are the essential preconditions, under this system, for the advancement of universal science in our environment. Until we can concentrate on decolonization, learn to nationalize our problems and take our poverty seriously, we shall continue to be both colonial and unoriginal. A national school, avowed and conscious, can perhaps add relevance, meaning and potency to our science; continued assent to the international system cannot.

References

Beals, Ralph L., "International Research Problems in Anthroplogy : a Report from the U.S.A.", *Current Anthropology,* 8: 5, 470-475, 1967.

Bose, Nirmal Kumar, *Fifty years of Science in India : Progress of Anthropology and Archaeology,* Calcutta: India Science Congress Association, 1963.

Fereira, John V., "Towards Integral Man through Integral Anthropology," *Sociological Bulletin,* 16:2, 77-93, 1967.

Levis-Strauss, Claude, "Anthropology : Its Achievements and Future," *Current Anthropology, 7 :* 2, 124-127, 1966.

Sturtevaun William C., "Urgent Anthropology : Smithsonian-Wenner-Gren Conference," *Current Anthropology,* 8: 4, 355-359, 1967.

7

ON SCHEMES OF RESEARCH AT INDIAN UNIVERSITIES

Rammanohar Lohia

[Lohia is primarily concerned with research in social sciences and humanities which he describes as "lesser romance of greater consequence." He believes research in arts has largely been descriptive not analytical. While descriptive research needn't be belittled, there ought to be greater emphasis on analytical research involving "bigger sectors and broader phases." Two interesting topics he suggests are land utilization in India, Asia and Europe, and place of women in Indian and foreign literatures. Another exciting project suggested by him is the comparative study of political parties – The Congress, the Kuomintang, Wafd – that have launched freedom struggle

*From *Interval During Politics,* ed. K.S. Karanth (Sindhu Publications, Bombay, 1987).

in various countries of Asia. Also, university men must subject European conceptual tools to thorough scrutiny and examine the validity of concepts like capitalism, Feudalism and Socialism etc. —Editor]

Among the main attraction of a university is the belief that it is the repository of wisdom and power and also of a purposeful curiosity which leads to more wisdom and power. A young mind is inflamed by the presence of this curiosity just as much as by that of athletics, of young and healthy bodies. The people profit from this romance of mind and body, from use of new territories of knowledge as from improvement of general health. Indian universities must make a forced-pace effort in either direction, as they have to start almost from scratch.

My intention at the moment is to confine myself to the romance of the mind. An almost sure recipe to awaken this romance is the presence of really learned teachers at the university, persons who know what there is to know of their subject and who can light up its main contours with special wit and wisdom. There will have to be greater reading of books and periodicals than is at present found among teachers. There will have to be much greater contemplation of the read material and of life. All of it, however, stays unsalted without the presence of notable research, of schemes and devotees of research, whose reputation is at least national, but preferably world-wide. The greater possible romance attaches to research, to systematic curiosity of the mind as wrests from darkness its region of beauty, power or wisdom.

Nothing hits the eye so much and is of such immediate consequence as research in the natural sciences. Such research in mathematics, chemistry, physics, geology and the like seems unmistakably to reveal mystery. I am not competent to talk about these schemes of research and their scientist except to say that, without them, a university of modern times must appear romanceless. The lesser romance of the social sciences is my immediate concern. In a sense, this lesser romance is of greater consequence, for its echoes reach the depths of mass consciousness and it provides partially the base on which the natural sciences are erected.

Research into social subjects should be mainly classified into that of the existing and the past, the modern and the ancient. The modern, in its turn, should be classified mainly into descriptive-analytical and theoretical-analytical. While the boundary lines between various subjects such as history, geography, literature, economics and mythology need not and should not be erased, there is need to coordinate all of them for purposes of research into a joint command with the three arms of the modern-descriptive, the modern-theoretical and the ancient.

Arts research at Indian universities has hitherto been largely modern-descriptive. Even there, it has confined itself to narrow sectors and transient phases. This is not to say that research, for instance, in the price indices or workers' conditions of a district or railway finances in the third or fourth decade of the century its unnecessary. Such research must go on. There is need, however, to take bigger sectors and broader phases, if the university wishes to become a true centre of the romance of the mind.

I may be permitted to illustrate. While land utilization in India is one such subject, it may lead on the one hand to fifteen similar enquiries of narrower but more intensive scope, and on the other to four or five of broader extent such as land utilization in Asia or Europe. The subject may also be split up into its various aspects of law, ownership, productive apparatus, pricing and the like, each with its own doctorate. Similar treatment may be given, for instance, to the place of woman in various literatures of India and outside or such emergent phenomena as non-violence or world-unity.

A vast and wonderful subject is opened up by emergent phenomena or such as are on the way out after having matured. Freedom of the coloured peoples has thrown up numerous such subjects. The agencies of this freedom like the Kuomintang, Wafd and the Congress have shown common features as also dissimilarities and such studies would not only yield the joy that belongs to all revelations of mysteries but could also gift wisdom.

While the Indian caste system may never fully open its mysteries to the researchist, its extension into existing professions of trade and industry provides a profitable field of enquiry. Such professions as boatmen, fishermen, water carriers and domestic servants belong, for instance, to a single broad caste and their present customs, rituals, ways of life and thought, in addition to their economic status and occupations, would yield rich material and some insights.

The descriptive-analytical must prepare the way for the theoretical-analytical, of which there is almost complete dearth at the Indian universities. Without research into the theoretical-analytical, enquiries of a descriptive kind must inevitably lose their value and become insipid dissertations for doctors of second-grade status and income. Particularly, must the enquiry into the theoretical-analytical become intense in non-European lands, as the conceptual tools of world-wide use are European in origin and validity. These tools must be subjected to a thorough enquiry. Their pretence at world-wide validity must be laid bare and the way must be prepared for better conceptual tools through fundamental analysis. It may not be fair to expect the candidate for doctorate, who is generally young and neither encyclopedic nor a genius, to fashion these tools. It would be more than fair to expect him to inspect these tools in their minute details and to list their value alongside of their inadequacies : Such research may well create the atmosphere, both within and outside the university, for the creation of tools of thought of universal validity.

Man's present thought is littered with such concepts of partial validity. They are, to list only some of them, 1. Progress, 2. Plenty, 3. Capitalism, 4. Feudalism, 5. Socialism or Communism. Each of these concepts is in continual use, both academic and conversational. Europe has so dominated the world's current thought that it does not occur to university men in the non-European world to submit these concepts to close examination. Like the team of blinkered oxen in an oil press, they go on and on researching into sectional conditions with Europe's tools and without a thought that these tools are inadequate and require to be refashioned.

Such abstractions as capitalism, communism or even socialism are indeed categories of thought that identify certain economic and social arrangements. They are at the same time and, even more so, unique historical phenomena incapable of reproduction without an identical setting. Communism is not merely abolition of private property. Has it been accomplished within the setting of mass production as in Czechoslovakia or agrarian stagnation as in Vietnam? Has it been accomplished within the setting of a low density of population as in Russia or a medium one as in China, not to talk of the setting of high density as in India? These two factors of population density and technological character are of such deciding importance that communism must indeed become wholly different creeds in accordance with the degree in which they are present. There is need therefore to examine these prevalent concepts of capitalism or communism. It may well be that their war of seeming extermination will be found on close inspection to be the rivalry of two wings of a common civilization. History and economics will then be understood not in Europe's terms of capitalism or communism but in the more universal terms of regional civilizations of varying periods.

Likewise, the concepts of plenty and progress require a most systematic and scientific examination. The superstition has been allowed to grow as though science has been causing a continual increase of progress and plenty or, at least, its benefactions are just around the corner. If steam or electricity or combustion oil has been unable to achieve forecasts made about it, humanity is not deterred from believing similar forecasts about atomic energy. There is certainly less food per head of the population in India and most areas of the coloured world that there was two thousand or some hundred years ago. But there is progress in the living standards of the upper middle classes of India and elsewhere and it is these who write books. Seekers of truth among university men need therefore to examine these concepts with great industry and insight. Adam Smith had the genius to equate international trade with geographical division of labour, a primarily British equation, but one that ruled the mind of the world for a hundred years and more.

J.M. Keynes had again the genius to add the concept of full employment to this equation, another British equation, but one that is currently ruling the mind of the English speaking world. University men in India should atleast strive to acquire that talent to examine all these concepts from inside as well as outside and attempt to discover the universal concept of comparatively equal productivity in all the world.

Alongside of the descriptive-analytical and the theoretical-analytical, there is need for a warm and intensive study of the ancient. All the world is at any moment the result of what it was in the past. India is par excellence, the result of the past. No country in the world lives in the abstractions, memories and legends of the past as does India. Men are moved to tears and joy and rioting over these affairs of the past easier than over current affairs. And yet there is no genuine study.

There was a Southern Highway in pre-history and, whether Ram walked over it in actuality or in legend, study must be made of it as of its successor in ancient Indian history. Likewise, the east-west highway of Krishna requires investigation. History, geography, literature and mythology must all pool their researches to make these subjects yield their mystery. Likewise, the story of Ganga, Narmada or

Kaveri in their past as in their current present will yield rich material. There has been a Sita of Valmiki as of Tulsidas, not to talk of folk-songs, and it would be rewarding to trace her career over the ages.

Some of these myths, symbols and abstractions continue into daily use and are causing much trouble and waste due to lack of knowledge. The India alphabets are an example. They are all variations of the Nagri alphabet. The Oriya alphabet, which appears at first sight so extraordinarily dissimilar to the Nagri, is in fact an extension of the same principle, which has made the Bengali alphabet somewhat different from the Nagri. The straight line tends to be replaced by increasingly curved and rounded lines. I would not be surprised if the history of the Tamil alphabet, whose sounds are the same as in Nagri, although of lesser number, disclosed similar features. India's languages need similarly to be studied in their detail as their broad and graphic sweep. The whole field of the ancient is littered with thousands of doctorates.

A university that undertakes an integrated programme of research in the descriptive-analytical, the theoretical-analytical and the ancient will have done well by the people of India. It will certainly have given a glamorous romance to itself. The mind of India will seek out such a university for its fulfillment. I need not add that the vehicle of such research can never be English. It must necessarily be Hindi or any of the other languages of India. I had at one time thought that postgraduate work in Indian universities must necessarily be carried out through the medium of Hindi. I must make a partial revision of this view. That sure touch in the handling of language, without which research in ancient subjects has absolutely no meaning and very little also in the descriptive or theoretical subjects, can alone be possible through the mother tongue. I hope the day will come when Hindustani shall be like a mother-tongue to all the children of India. But, until that day comes all languages of India should be accepted as medium for post-graduate research. Otherwise, the voluminous and insipid size of present doctorates, largely enforced because of a medium with which the researchist is not at home, will continue.

8

THEIR CLASSICS, OUR CLASSICS

Ashok Celly

[The celebrated texts of the western world are primarily concerned with issues that relate to their culture and cannot have the kind of significance for Indian academics they have for their western counterparts. The central intellectual concerns of Weber's *The Protestant Ethic and The Rise of Capitalism and* Marcuse's *Eros and Civilization* are discussed to substantiate the argument. This does not, however, mean that the western texts are altogether irrelevant and must be discarded. Only their relevance is not a donne a given: it is more a matter of inference and application. Similarly our ancient texts like Kautliya's *Arthasastra* and Bharat's *Natyasastra* – our classics – don't belong to a dead past. In fact, they help us to understand different facets of our culture and hence are of interest not just to the specialists but also others with a broader interest in our culture. Hence their retrieval must be a legitimate part of our intellectual project.
–Editor]

Thanks to the political domination of the British and introduction of western learning in India, we also imbibed the Baconian ideal of infinite knowledge. As a consequence their celebrated texts acquired as much significance for us as they had for the western academia. Any questioning of this belief was dismissed as xenophobia or intellectual provincialism. That knowledge had a socio-cultural dimension, that most intellectual, if not all, activity had its roots in the socio-cultural milieu was lost sight of. So their classics became our classics and our classics went into oblivion. For interestingly enough the fact that western scholars were mostly concerned with their culture and its intellectual products didn't seem to bother us. The situation is not very different today.

Here I propose to show that their celebrated intellectual texts have little or limited relevance to our socio-cultural situation. However, this is not to say they should be discarded; only they be read and made use of more critically. Their relevance is not a given, a donne. Every western text must be scrutinised from this standpoint, i.e., its relevance to our culture, our society and our ecoomy. The old colonial reverence—and it largely persists even today — must give way to scepticism born of self-esteem and intellectual self-confidence.

My first example is Max Weber's *Rise of Capitalism and The Protestant Ethic* a book which enjoys the reputation of being a *magnum opus* written by one of the greatest sociologists of all times, Weber's book is specifically concerned with the rise of capitalism in the west and sees an intimate connection between its growth and what he calls the Protestant ethic. Weber marshals enormous evidence to show that "business leaders and owners of skill, as well as the higher grades of skilled labour, and even more the higher technically and commercially trained personnel of modern enterprise are overwhelmingly protestant."[1] Also, the work offers a brilliant portrait of the capitalist mind and argues that the protestant ethic with its asceticism, its deification of labour and its distrust of "the spontaneous enjoyment of life"[2] acted as a powerful impetus for the growth of capitalism in the west. It not only restricted consumption but also had the effect of freeing the acquisition of goods from the inhibition of traditionalist ethics.

Weber's book was hailed as a great intellectual event in the west and understandably so. Here was a totally different perspective on capitalism—different from that of Karl Marx. It highlighted the cultural factors that were responsible for the rise of capitalism, something that had been ignored or belittled by Marx and his colleague Engels. No wonder, the sociologists sat up and took notice and the 'protestant ethic' became a part of the lexicon of the western intellectual

But what pray is its relevance to the understanding of a culture like India which is essentially a non-Christian country? Obviously, it can have no direct relevance to the understanding of our socio-cultural situation. In other words the significance of the Weber's book could serve as a useful starting point for intellectual exploration on the following lines. Is the absence of the Protestant ethic in any way responsible for the retarded growth of capitalism in India? An alternative line of inquiry could be : Is there an Indian analogue of the Protestant ethic? For instance are the entrepreneurial abilities of, say, the Parsis or the Marwaris in some way related to their philosophy of life, their 'ethic' in Weberian terminology. If some sociological investigations have been conducted on these lines, I am not aware of them.

Let us now look at another celebrated text of the western world —a text that deals with a philosophical theme of universal appeal, namely, *Eros and Civilization* by Herbert Marcuse. Starting with the Freudian definition of civilization as repression, Marcuse contends that civilization needn't be essentially repressive as Freud feared. Marcuse makes a distinction between basic repression and surplus repression. (One can detect the influence of Karl Marx there). While the former refers to the repression of "instincts necessary for the perpetuation of the human race in civilization, the latter denotes the quantum of repression necessitated by "the prevailing historical form of the reality principle." In other words there was a good deal of repression which was caused by an oppressive socio-economic system, i.e., capitalism and could be eliminated. Marcuse thus envisages a non-repressive civilization—a civilization made possible by the very achievements of capitalism, that is, material prosperity, automation and reduction of the working day etc. In such a civilization work will not be a neurotic necessity and will be replaced by play or work itself will become a mode of play. "...the human body would become an instrument of pleasure rather than labour."[5]

The social context of Marcuse's theorising is essentially western, that is, a capitalist society with a high level of economic prosperity. I am afraid that cannot of be much relevance to what has come to be known as the third world including India. For notwithstanding the existence of a 100 million strong middle class in India, this part of the world still consists primarily of 'the wretched of the earth,' for whom work and toil is the supreme fact of existence and all their energy goes into making two ends meet. As far as they are concerned the kind of scenario Marcuse envisages can only be a dream or dreamfare doled out by Bollywood.

E.H. Carr's *What is History?* is even more instructive. Admittedly, Carr is no John Bull. Far from it. He in fact makes a plea for "the widening horizon" and denounces the British universities for their Eurocentric bias (which incidentally lends support to the point I made earlier, i.e., in practice only western knowledge is considered universal). Carr observes, "A candidate possessing knowledge of the affairs of Asia, Africa or Latin America has at present a very limited opportunity of displaying it in a paper called with magnificent nineteenth century panache 'The Expansion of Europe.' The title unfortunately fits the contents. The candidate is not invited to know anything even of countries with an important and well-documented history like China or Persia, except *What happened when the Europeans attempted to take them over* (italics mine)."

Yet ironically enough Carr conducts his argument exclusively in the context of British or European history picking up all his examples from one or the other. The nineteenth century indifference to the philosophy of history is related to the fact that "for the intellectuals of western Europe, it was a comfortable period exceeding confidence and optimism." And the event in Carr's opinion which brought about a change in the historian's approach was the First World War which was essentially a European affair. With all his radicalism Carr makes no reference whatsoever to an Asian thinker or a historical event in that part of the globe. And that in a discussion of so fundamental a nature.

Such instances can be multiplied. Elizabeth Lawrence's *The Origins and Growth of Modern Education,* is supposed to deal with the history of education from Plato to Piaget, but it does not have a word about Gandhi or Tagore the two significant educational thinkers of India, even Asia. John Passamore's *A Hundered Years of Philosophy* a popular text book is written, as the author concedes in the preface, "from an English Point of view so far as that is possible for an Australian"[8] English point of view! Here is a classic case of 'Colonial' empathy. It sums up the tragedy of the third world in a nutshell (even though Australia does not exactly belong there). Internalising the consciousness of the white man and abdicating their own identity. And Karl Papper the eminent British political thinker declares at the very outset that his work *The Open Society and Its Enemies*—once a hot favourite with the students and teachers of Political Science in India—"sketches some of the difficulties faced by *Our Civilization*"[9] (italics mine). That is to say their civilization, not ours. The refrain is heard all the time. But we seem to have lost all sense of reality, even dignity and persist in what seems to be a crazy and somewhat sterile enterprise.

II

It is not enough to place the western 'classics' in their socio-cultural context and denude them of their mythical universality. It is equally important to recognize our intellectual heritage, to know the past, to discover and critique our classics. To know the past is to know one's strengths and weaknesses, which in turn helps us to determine our future priorities. To know the past is not necessarily to become enslaved to it as some people are inclined to believe; in fact, it would enable us to get rid of its dead wood. Also, it should help us to trace the roots of our aspirations and thus provide strength for our collective endeavours. Change is best possible by making friends with tradition, *parampara*. As Professor Kantak puts it, "............. without a proper appreciation of the achievements of our past we might continue to be inhibited in our ability to be innovative and to be ourselves in the model world."[10] A radical break with the past is either very superficial or invites a fundamentalist backlash.

And the past, to a very large extent, lies buried in our classics. To read Manusmriti, for instance, is to become aware of the roots of the Hindu social structure. The oppressive nature of our caste-system, particularly its anti-shudra and anti-woman bias, can be traced to *The Laws of Manu,* that is, *Manusmriti.* Perhaps it would be more appropriate to say, to the times of Manu. Also to read Manusmriti is to become aware that there is nothing sacrosanct or eternal about the Hindu social structure, for at least women in pre-Manu India enjoyed equality with men and a Gargi or a Maitreyi could hold her own against the very best male scholars of the land. As Lannoy observes in *The Speaking True,* "Pre-Manu India accorded women equality with men in the Vedic sacrifice. At that time women could become priests; there was no immolation of the widow on her husband's funer pyre (Sati), and widows were allowed to remarry. The Vedic age was more liberal in its attitude towards women than the long period following the composition of the *Laws of Manu* which, become the canon law of Hinduism."[11]

Again, *Manusmriti* acquaints us with the political agenda of the Brahmins, namely, to establish their hegemony over people who have power of arms and wealth. "The Laws of Manu may well have been inspired by the desire to establish Brahmin status over physical force (Ksatriyas) and economic power (Vaisyas)......."[12]

Manusmriti thus becomes our window on an extremely vital segment of history and in the process plays a liberating role - liberating us from the tyranny of absolutes. Isn't that the business of historical consciousness? The most powerful Dalit formation in India - the Bahujan Samaj Party (BSP)—denounces all mainstream political parties as Manuvadi thereby establishing the relevance of Manu who generates intense emotions. Therefore one may condemn *Manusmriti* as diabolic or retrograde but one cannot deny its relevance even today.

Similarly, Kautilya's *Arthashastra* is an important book not only for students of Indian political thought—these intellectual milestones cannot be pigeonholed—it is also an important text for sociologists and historians.

For one—the sort of political scenario it depicts it is not very different from ours—intrigues, manipulation and the lust for power etc. This is the world of realpolitik *par excellence*. Two, it is refreshingly modunistic in the sense that it recognises the primary of the science of government in man's societal existence. Three, it provides the necessary antidote to the romantic scenario that the traditionalists like to conjure of the past when the king was a selfless, dedicated servant of the people in the manner of the hero of *The Ramayana* and seers and scholars are seen as engaged in the exalted pursuit of knowledge. In a word, *Arthasashtra* by de-idolising our past helps us to understand it better recognize the links that exist between the past and the present.

The irony is while foreign scholars have recognized it as a significant political text, Indian scholars afraid to be labeled obscurantist (so much for intellectual daring !) are reluctant to do so. Richard Lannoy, known for his serious engagement with India's culture, pays a glorious tribute to the originality of Kautilya's Artha-Shastra. "The daring originality of this difficult, complex work is unquestioned, the nature of its novel thinking is nevertheless firmly set within the large scheme of *dharma*. Kautilya has been compared with Machiavelli in this respect; from the similarities and their differences much useful clarification can be obtained. The *Arthastastra* was written approximately eighteen hundred years before the publication of *The Prince*...."[13]

Again, students of literature and fine arts (like music and dance) need to be conversant with Bharat's *Natya Shastra* to break free of the stranglehold of western/Aristotolian poetics. They must know there are works like Kalidasa's *Shakuntalam* and Bhasa's Uttarrancharitam whose beauty and grandeur are not accessible though western canons of art.

Also, to be acquainted with Indian poetics in general and *Natya Shastra* in particular is able to understand the intimate relationship in our culture between drama on the one hand and dance and music on the other which makes it a very different kettle of fish from that of the west. To quote Professor Kantak who is equally at home with European and Sanskrit literature, "Firstly there is the peculiar integration of music, poetry, dance and drama as in the Bharat *Natyasastra.* Dance and drama are indeed so close that the rootword for drama Nata is supposed to be the Prakrit form of Nrt meaning to dance"[14]. Also, the extraordinary emphasis on dance and music helps us to understand the peculiar genius of Indian cinema and its affinity with Sanskrit.

Above all the acquaintance with Indian poetics along with that of the west should help us to acquire a more balanced perspective. It should enable us to resist the tendency to hierarchies works of art - notions like Shakespeare is the greatest and western literature is superior to that of the east etc. and thus free us from intellectual provincialism. However one needs to guard equally against xenophobia and self-glorification at the same time. (Kalidasa is the greatest and the best ideas have had their origin in India and so on.)

Then there is the entire corpus of the indigenous system of medicine known as Ayurveda which at one time was dismissed as unscientific, so much mumbo-jumbo. The truth, however, is that it is one of the oldest systems of medicine the world has known, that Charak and Susruta were the great pioneers in the world of medicine, and observation and experiment were the twin basis of the science of healthy living called Ayurveda.

Susant Goontilake the formidable Sri Lankan scholar, in the pathbreaking work *Towards Global Science,* has decisively established the highly empirical nature of this enterprise, "The classical writers Charak and Susruta... advised medical practitioners to ask those who spent much of their time in the forest - shepherds, goatherds, fowlers and ascetics—about useful plants and drugs. This, we should recall, is the exact methodology being followed by pharmaceutical companies when they search for effective cures among indigenous peoples in the Amazon forest..."[15]

Shehnaj Husain the herbal 'queen' owes her spectacular success and international reputation entirely to Ayurveda as she herself admitted in an interview with *The Times of India.* "In the past 25 years I have been doing nothing but trying to reproduce in bottles and jars wisdom distilled from ancient Indian texts. Uptill now we have produced 50 products all of whom have been sure-fire success, and all based on prescriptions given in Ayurved."[16] Can there be a greater tribute to a system of medicine?

References

1. *The Protestant Ethic and the Spirit of Capitalism* (London : Routledge & Kegan Paul, 1996), p. 35.
2. *Ibid.*, p. 53.
3. *Eros and Civilization* (London : Sphere Books, 1969), p. 44.
4. *Ibid.*, p. 44.
5. Political Preface 1966, *Eros and Civilization*, p. 13.
6. *What is History* (Penguin : Harmondsworth, 1964), p. 151.
7. *Ibid.*, p. 19.
8. *A Hundred Years of Philosophy.*
9. Introduction, *The Open Society and Its Enemies* (London : Routledge & Kegan Paul, 1945, 1977), p. 1.
10. "In Search of Valid Response to Literature" in *Perspectives On Indian Literary Culture* (Pencraft International, Delhi, 1996), p. 31.
11. *The Speaking Tree* (London: Oxford University Press, 1971), pp. 102-03.
12. Introduction to *The Laws of Manu,* trans. Wendy Doniger with Brian K. Smith. (London: Penguin, 1991) p. XLVII.

13. *The Speaking Tree,* p. 316.
14. "On the Misreading of Kalidasa and Shakespeare" in *Perspectives on Indian Literary Culture,* p. 115.
15. *Toward A Global Science - Mining Civilizational Knowledge* (Vistaar Publications), N. Delhi, 1998), p. 83.
16. Interview to *The Times of India,* Nov. 11, 1998.

BIBLIOGRAPHY

Altabch, Philip G. *Higher Education in the Third World.* Radiant Publishers, New Delhi,1987.

Altabch, Philip G. & Kelly Gail P. *Education and Colonialism.*Longman, London and New York,1987.

Alvares, Claude. *Decolonizing History — Technology and Culture in India, China and the West.* New York: Apex Press, Goa: The other India, 1991.

Aron, Raymond. *Main Currents in Sociological Thought,* Vol. 2. Harmondsworth: Penguin, 1970, rpt 1976.

Ashby, Eric. *Universities : British, Indian, African.* London: Weidenfeld & Nicolson.

Atal, Yogesh (ed.). *S.C. Dube on Crisis and Commitment in Social Sciences.* New Delhi: Abhinav Publications, 1983.

Carr, E.H. *What is History?* Harmondsworth: Penguin, 1961, rpt. 1975.

Curtin, Philip D. *Imperialism.* London and Basingstoke: Macmillan, 1971.

Daya Krishna (ed.) *India's Intellectual Traditions.* Delhi: Indian Council of Philosophical Research & Motilal Banarsidas, 1987.

Gay, Peter. *The Enlightenment: An Interpretation.* London: Weidenfeld and Nicolson, 1966.

Ghose, Sisirkumar (ed.). *Four Indian Critical Essays.* Calcutta: Jijnasa, 1977.

Goontilake, Susantha. *Towards a Global Science — Mining Civilization Knowledge.* Vistaar Publications, New Delhi, 1998.

Heller, Erich. *The Importance of Nietzsche.* Chicago: The University of Chicago Press, 1988.

Joshi, P.C. *Social Science and Development: quest for relevance.* Har-Anand Publications, New Delhi, 1995.

Kantak, V.Y. *Perspectives on Indian Literary Culture.* Pencraft International, Delhi, 1996.

Kumar Dharma & Mookherjee, Dilip (eds.). *D. School.* Oxford University Press, Delhi, 1995.

Lannoy, Richard. *The Speaking Tree — A study of Indian Culture and Society.* London: Oxford University Press, 1971.

Marcuse, Herbert. *Eros And Civilization.* London: Sphere Books Ltd, 1969.

Maxwell, Nicholes. *From Knowledge to Wisdom — A Revolution in the Aims & Methods of Science.* Oxford: Basil Balckwell, 1984.

Murphy, Timothy. *Nietzsche As Educator.* Lanham, New York & London: University Press of America, 1984.

Nietzsche. *Twilight Of The Idols* and *The Anti-Christ* trans. R.J. Hollingdale. Harmondsworth: Penguin, 1968, rpt. 1981.

----------- *Untimely Meditations,* trans. R.J. Hollingdale. Cambridge: Cambridge University Press, 1983.

Ngugi wa Thiongo. *Decolonizing the Mind — The Politics of Language in African Literature.* London: James Curry, 1986.

Paranjape, Makrand. *Decolonization and Development — Hind Svaraj Revisited.* Sage Publications, New Delhi, 1993.

Popper, K.R. *The Open Society And Its Enemies,* Vol. I. London: Routledge & Kegan Paul, 1945, 1977.

Rudolp LIoyd & Ruldolph Susanne. *The Modernity of Tradition — Political Development in India.*Chicago: University of Chicago Press, 1967.

Said, Edward. *Orientalism.* London: Routledge & Kegan Paul, 1978.

Singh, Amrik & Sharma G.D. (eds.). *Higher Education in India.* Konark, New Delhi, 1988.

Shils, Edward. *Centre and Periphery — Essays in Macrosociology.* Chicago: University of Chicago Press, 1975.

Tagore, Rabindranath. *Selections from the Works of Rabindranath Tagore*. Bombay: Macmillan & Co, 1946.

Visvanthan, Gauri. *Masks of Conquest: Literary Study and British Rule in India*. London: Faber & Faber, 1990.

Watt, Ian. *Myths of Modern Individualism*. Cambridge: Cambridge University Press, 1996.

Weber, Max. *The Protestant Ethic and The Spirit of Capitalism*. London: Routledge & Kegan Paul, 1962, rpt, 1996.

INDEX

C+Yan